WHAT PEOPLE ARE SAYING ABOUT

THE GIFT OF AN ANGEL

I don't normally read books on angels as I find many of them too saccharine, but I found Wendy Erlick's book *The Gift of an Angel* direct, authentic and sometimes very moving. Wendy has a knack of expressing profound truths simply, and her book should appeal to beginners and advanced spiritual workers alike.

Cilla Conway, author and creator of *The Intuitive Tarot*, and the *Devas of Creation* cards

This is a book to grace any bookshelf of anyone interested in practical, everyday spirituality and in making a personal connection with the angelic realm. An easy read and very inspiring.

Colin Tipping, author, *Radical Forgiveness: A Revolutionary Five-Stage Process to Heal Relationships, Let Go of Anger and Blame, Find Peace in Any Situation*

A wonderful inspiring and heartwarming story.

Michael Mann, publisher, Watkins Books

Wendy is a talented angel channeler whose authentic voice promotes intuition, love and healing.

Etan Ilfeld, owner, Watkins Books

The Gift
of an Angel

A Journey to Integrating Spirituality
Into Everyday Life

The Gift
of an Angel

A Journey to Integrating Spirituality
Into Everyday Life

Wendy Jane Erlick

BOOKS

Winchester, UK
Washington, USA

First published by O-Books, 2016
O-Books is an imprint of John Hunt Publishing Ltd., Laurel House, Station Approach,
Alresford, Hants, SO24 9JH, UK
office1@jhpbooks.net
www.johnhuntpublishing.com

For distributor details and how to order please visit the 'Ordering' section on our website.

Text copyright: Wendy Jane Erlick 2015
Cover and author photo by Tracy Byles-Walker

ISBN: 978 1 78535 005 4
Library of Congress Control Number: 2015946044

A CIP catalogue record for this book is available from the British Library.

Design: Stuart Davies

Printed and bound by CPI Group (UK) Ltd, Croydon, CR0 4YY, UK

We operate a distinctive and ethical publishing philosophy in all
areas of our business, from our global network of authors to
production and worldwide distribution.

CONTENTS

Dedicated:

For my sons Josh and Zack for being with me on this journey.

Acknowledgements

This book would not have been possible without the support of family, friends and colleagues.

Sincere appreciation goes to the owners of Watkins Media, Etan Ilfeld and Marianna Ilfeld, for their support and belief in my Divine abilities; to my Editor and friend Leah Kotkes for being a miracle in my life; to Michael Mann, publisher of Watkins Media for his early encouragement; to Elizabeth Radley of O-Books for her speedy and comprehensive editing; to all of the staff of Watkins Books for their kindness and encouragement; to Tobe Aleksander for initial editing, and suspension of personal belief and organization; to Melinda Tenty for rescuing me many times with kindness and without judgment; to her daughter Natasha for being patient; to Shelley Dorfmann and Berl Goldbart for their sound friendship and practical support; to Raphaela Cooper for believing in me from the beginning; to Tracey Byles-Walker for amazing and unstintingly generous support and friendship; to Alison Abrams for helping to restore me to myself; to Ivan and Denise Green for giving me a space in which to write; to Eamon and Alison Osment for looking after our dog Lily while I was writing; to Peter Bently and Lucy Curtin for helping me write the first synopsis; to Marianna Komarovsky for Skype Healing when needed; to my friend and colleague Jugal Sharma and his wife Audrey for their integrity and support that has spanned many decades. To Ruth and David Willis for thirty years of friendship through thick and thin as well as this book; to Kim and David Howard for friendship, plus encouragement; to Sue Matto for many cups of coffee; to Liam Scales for patient kindness; to Helen Erlick for her act of generosity; to my mother Barbara for encouraging me to follow my dreams.

Presently the Mage said, speaking softly, "Do you see, Arren, how an act is not, as young men think, like a rock that one picks up and throws, and it hits or misses, and that's the end of it. When that rock is lifted the earth is lighter, the hand that bears it heavier. When it is thrown the circuits of the stars respond, and where it strikes or falls the universe is changed. On every act the balance of the whole depends. The winds and seas, the powers of water and earth and light, all that these do, and all that the beasts and green things do, is well done and rightly done. All these act within the Equilibrium. From the hurricane and the great whale's sounding to the fall of a dry leaf and the gnat's flight, all they do is done within the balance of the whole. But we, in so far as we have power over the world and over one another, we must *learn* to do what the leaf and the whale and the wind do of their own nature. We must learn to keep the balance. Having choice we must not act without responsibility. Who am I – though I have the power to do it – to punish and reward, playing with men's destinies?"

"Mage Light", page 361, *The Earthsea Quartet* by Ursula Le Guin (Penguin, 1993)[1]

Preface

"Dearest One,

You must write your book as soon as it is possible; there is urgency to the message contained within. It is needed to bring light and give hope.

Although you do not recognize the fact you have been courageous, this book will have contained within it the potential to allow other people to shine, to speak their truth and find their own courage in supporting the Divine.

'*The Great Shift*' that you personally will experience in early 2013 will prepare you and also grant you the abilities to support and guide those that come to you to undergo their own transitions. This time of change will be a difficult but crucial time of change that will benefit you greatly; and in time others who you help will come to their own realizations about the worth and the advantages associated to their own transition. You will be an inspiration to all those that seek you; you will support and comfort them as they make the inevitable transition from material to spiritual and then find their sense of priority and balance between the two realms. For in our generation and the future the two realms have to coexist; the world can no longer be led by materialism alone.

Step into your power and truth in order to assist others. Many humans are suffering and are confused as they shift the dimension of their experience to integrate the material and the spiritual. They believe that they are disconnected and alone. This is not the case. Your purpose is to remind them of the abundance and joy. Every person is a miracle. Every person has the right to dance in his or her power. Each person has the right to laughter in his or her lives."

Channeled Message to me from my Personal Angel Celestial Bell, July 2012, Devon, England

The Gift of an Angel interweaves two stories, the story of my personal journey to *accepting* and *utilizing* my psychic ability, and the exploration of the channeled messages I have received all my life.

Until July 2012, when I received a channeled message from my Personal Angel advising me to write this book, I had resisted a working relationship with the psychic world and the responsibility that accompanies it; all my life I had been in conflict with this gift I knew I had which I had attributed to God's grace.

Until I altered my attitude and adopted a professional attitude to this gift and undertook years of accredited training to equip myself by authenticating my skills, I could not undertake the role of an Energy Healer, Angel Reader and Intuitive Coach.

Misunderstanding as well as ridicule surrounds the topic of Psychic or Divine Intervention and Spiritual Mysticism. This negative and misguided mindset has eroded authentic spirituality; its meaning, purpose and effect. *The Gift of an Angel* invites you to experience a professional and truthful account of the world that exists around us and within us in relation to the integration of spirituality in the material and rational world.

This is a book about what happened when I began to listen to my own Personal Angel. When I invested time and energy to make this unique relationship work for me that I did through introspection, acknowledgement, professional training and service. In doing so, I have gained the ability to guide and serve a growing number of people from all walks of life who are conscientiously looking to live life in a different way than they did before; a life where spirituality and regard for the needs of their heart and soul are equal to their material and physical needs; where an investment in the spiritual and emotional aspects of their well-being is equal to if not more of a priority than superficial material wants and desires.

Today, I have a new purpose to my life. I am an Energy Healer, Angel Reader and Intuitive Coach. By accepting the gift God gave me, that of my own Personal Angel, I now work with my Angel and in doing so I have secured my place in the world. In turn, I am able to help others secure and enjoy their place in their own lives. This is my story and I hope it inspires and helps you.

Once my life was ordinary, on a regular basis I was challenged by obstacles and concerns, and like most people I let worries and disappointments pull me down emotionally. But all through those regular days with their many challenges I was blessed with an Angel who was doing her best to make herself known to me because my Angel wanted to help me; to guide and support me. It was not until 2009 that I finally decided to team up with my own Personal Angel and embark on a new way to live my life.

Becoming a collaborative partner with my Angel changed my life; a harmonious relationship ensued which has not only augmented and enriched my life but helped me show others how to do the same.

When I recognized and accepted my psychic ability my life changed for the better. It took time for me to acknowledge I had psychic abilities. When I did, overnight I was empowered and my life became extraordinary.

Today, just like everyone around me, I have challenges, and sometimes things happen that are upsetting, but now I am more resilient. I have a 24-hour support system in my Personal Angel; this gives me incredible peace of mind.

Today, I have a secure resource for myself, which also allows me to offer the same support to others. I also have a professional life in association with my closest confidante and intimate, my Personal Angel.

Today, I wake each morning with gratitude for the spiritual work that I am able to do, that gives insight and guidance to others while it sustains and guides me.

Today, I no longer journey on the road of life alone. I travel with a loyal companion who I can turn to for support and guidance, and in turn I can share what I know and my resources with others. I thank God each day for bringing me to this knowingness because I love the work that I do. I love the fact God granted me with my psychic abilities and my innate spiritual gifts, and that I have a worthy purpose in this world.

I hope the story of my spiritual transition and empowerment gives you hope to realize this can also be your story. I hope one day we meet and share stories that are both inspiring and as magical as the story I want to tell you now.

Part One
Ordinary Life

He spoke softly and his eyes were sombre as he looked at Ged. You thought, as a boy, that a Mage is one who can do anything. So I thought once. So did we all. And the truth is that as a man's real power grows and his knowledge widens ever the way he can follow grows narrower; until at last he chooses nothing, but does only and wholly what he must do…

"The Loosing of the Shadow", page 73, *The Earthsea Quartet* by Ursula Le Guin (Penguin, 1993)

Chapter One

I was born in April 1960. A Silver Rope accompanied me throughout my childhood. This is how it all started and ended.

I grew up in Loughton, in Essex, an English county that is close to London but in the early 1960s was still unspoiled, rural countryside. We lived high on a hill, at the end of a terrace of houses that barely constituted a street. From my bedroom window I could see the rooftop of the home of my paternal grandparents. They lived above their corner shop that sold everything from household items to groceries; they had cultivated a large vegetable garden behind the shop for their own use. Further in the distance, I could see the smaller rooftop of the home of my maternal grandparents. I was close to and loved all the members of my extended family that included two uncles and four aunts.

I was born to my mother two weeks after her twenty-first birthday in the army hospital in Fleet, near to Aldershot, Surrey. I can remember feeling very happy when I was a small child; in fact my earliest childhood memory dates back to age one or two. I can clearly remember branches of trees and the movement of dappled sunshine. After I was born my mother had moved from the army barracks in Aldershot and brought me back to Loughton. We lived in a one-bedroom beige caravan in the large vegetable garden behind the corner shop of my paternal grandparents, Albert and Florence. I was the first grandchild, doted on by all my grandparents. I had the freedom to roam in the garden when I liked; I loved that garden. My father visited when he was on leave from his regiment. This period of time was a life of peace and plenty.

My happy life came to an abrupt end when I was three years old; my eldest brother was born. It was not only the displacement of being the adored only child in the family that caused me consternation, but the loss of freedom. We moved to an apartment in another location far from the vegetable garden where I could no longer run around as free as a bird. My parents were allocated a flat by social housing in a rougher area closer to London, far from my grandparents and their love. As far as I was concerned I was incarcerated; rightfully so, I was not permitted to leave the flat by myself in this urban location but I felt my wings were clipped at a very young age. I also dearly missed the company and kindness of four wonderful grandparents and my lively aunts and uncles.

While we were living in this urban flat there was an incident that I do not wish to disclose in its entirety; it is enough to say it caused me to feel completely terrified of one of my parents and, I now realize unfairly, betrayed by the other. At the time of this incident I made a conscious decision that I did not wish to live with my parents but, of course, I had no choice; therefore subconsciously I deliberately detached from relating to them. I lived a very depressed life from that point onwards; I didn't care if I lived or died. Because I did not wish to incur any issue with my parents that would shake my world, I kept to myself and did whatever I had to do to go from A to B until bedtime.

My first brother was born in 1963, another brother in 1965 and my youngest in 1968. By now we had returned to Loughton, Essex. Times were tough economically for our family. After my father fulfilled his duties in the Parachute Regiment of the British Army he became an ice cream man. Ice cream trade was better in the summer than in the winter; therefore the money flow in our house was erratic. Conditions improved marginally when my father obtained work as a milkman; this was not seasonal work, and it also meant that then we had fresh milk daily in the house and double cream on Sundays. Full credit goes to my mother; with ingenuity she was able to stretch any provision we had that little bit further.

When I was not in school I could usually be found in the home of my maternal grandparents or working for a salary in my grandmother Florence's corner shop. In this way I felt protected by my extended family. This situation suited me because I had this great need to be away from our family home.

At home, I was allocated the role of 'helping Mum look after the boys' but I resisted this role at every opportunity. I was an avid reader and a frequent library-goer; reading was my comfort and my escape from being a 'child carer' before 'my time'. I would call into the library and would take my full quota of books out at one go, twelve at a time, and 'consume' them; read at every available moment in my bedroom. When I was not at my grandparents' or reading I could be found walking in the nearby Epping Forest, a beautiful place that I regarded as my respite. I did not watch television or listen to music. It was too chaotic in our home with my three younger brothers and all of the 'business' flying between my parents.

My oases of peace and safety were the homes of my grandparents and I loved them. But my best source of support and comfort and strength was a glowing Silver Rope that I saw in the etheric; it appeared and helped me when I truly needed it. It came into my life one day in my fifth year. I was walking along the street in Loughton, Essex, with my mother; we were far from anything familiar to me. She pushed a large carriage pram of which she was very proud. It had been bought for me at great expense just after I had been born. Now it contained two of my brothers: one a baby, the other a toddler. My mother had informed us we were going to walk a long way; there was somewhere she needed to go, something urgent she needed to do. I remember feeling cold and hungry. I was an empathetic child, fully aware of my mother's emotions; of her despair, anger and dismay at our poverty-stricken and difficult situation. I cannot now remember where we were going, all that I can recall is I did not want to walk anywhere. It was very bad weather and I was very tired; I did not feel I had the strength to go anywhere.

A terrible feeling consumed me: I saw no reason at all to live; I had full knowledge of our situation and hated it.

In hindsight, I think I absorbed all my mother's feelings into my small soul and I could not contain what was happening. My despair was so great I think God took compassion on me, and heard the prayer I was calling out inside of my head. I was begging God to take me home; I was feeling very scared and getting more and more upset.

Suddenly, a Silver Rope appeared before me, just like that! The Silver Rope ran out of my tummy and extended as far as I could see into the space ahead of me. The Silver Rope had a double light around it like a halo. It was perfectly straight, about twenty or so feet in length. When I was five, I recall not seeing where it disappeared to but it seemed to be pulling me in the direction we were going. As soon as we arrived at our destination the Rope disappeared. I didn't tell anyone about the Silver Rope; like Alice when she fell down the rabbit hole in Lewis Carroll's *Alice's Adventures in Wonderland*. I didn't see the experience as anything out of the ordinary. But from that day onwards whenever I was in real need throughout my childhood the Silver Rope would suddenly appear and pull me along. This Silver Rope gave me an enormous boost of support; an energy that radiated out of me but was part of me and filled my body with hope. I loved it whenever the Silver Rope appeared; the feeling it gave me was that I was sure everything would be all right, whenever it was there. I had this experience with the Silver Rope until I was sixteen.

When I was sixteen years old I met Adam* who became my boyfriend. Adam's mother welcomed me into her home like a daughter. The family lived in Chigwell, Essex. Adam's family were Jewish. His mother kept a kosher home; the family ethic was born out of a strong sense of Jewish identity and pride. I felt instantly welcome and appreciated in Adam's home; I felt safe and respected.

The Silver Rope stopped appearing when I met Adam: I think

because I had found a safe haven and also I was learning how to look after myself and go where I needed to go to get what was best for me and my future. I left for university two years later when I was eighteen. Adam's family was responsible for introducing me to a new way of looking at life, for totally changing my outlook on family values and loving-kindness.

Looking back on my childhood now that I am a mother myself, I can see that my own mother had been greatly challenged and suffered dearly. Within it all, she was able to give me enough love and the freedom to extricate myself. I was the first child of my family to go to university. She encouraged me to do so; she wanted me to have a chance of being economically independent through a good quality education. I am grateful to her for this vision. And the meaning and purpose behind the Silver Rope? In hindsight, I wonder if it was just that at five years of age I was lucky enough to be able to see that which every human being has: an umbilical cord to the Divine to help see us through all of our days.

*Name changed to protect privacy.

Chapter Two

It is the autumn of 1979. I am a student at the University of Hull in the north of England. I am reading Sociology and Social Anthropology; it is my second year. I am nineteen years old. I am a member of the Hull University Fell Walking and Rambling Association. Around eighty people meet monthly and take an excursion to a popular walking trail; we travel to the starting point of each walk by coach.

I am sitting on the side of the road in the Yorkshire Dales, an area of outstanding natural beauty about fifty miles from the university campus. I can feel a light chilly wind coming up from the dip in the valley. It is around 10am. It is a damp and misty morning. The air is chilled, sharp. There is confusion and chaos around me: screaming, distress. The two-coach excursion has turned into a nightmare; our coach slipped on agricultural mud and turned onto its roof. Thankfully I managed to crawl out of a smashed window. The coach behind us managed to make an emergency stop. At this moment, every able-bodied person is trying to turn the coach back on to an even footing. No emergency services have arrived yet. There is a dense atmosphere with energy of subdued shock. I am disorientated; I was sleeping when the coach crashed. I am fully alert now, watching, but I cannot move. An excruciating pain shoots down my back. Am I in a dream? I don't understand what is going on.

I look at the upside down coach. Above the wheels and base of the coach is a bright iridescent rainbow light. Silvery white humanlike forms that resemble what I assume must be Angels; a vortex of light streaming through reaches out hands towards the roof of the coach.

Today, I know now that I saw Angelic forms, welcoming the souls of the people that were dead under the coach. But at the time, in the autumn of 1979 I did not know what was going on;

all I saw was this magnificent scene of beauty and Angelic activity. The pleas of the passengers ebbed and flowed because I also heard a sound of music that to be honest I have no words to describe; the only reference that I can give it now is that it was classical in tone and cantorial. Oddly, in the midst of this horrific scene of mayhem I could palatably feel a heightened sense of anticipation and joy. From the ground where I sat I also felt a throbbing sensation. I wanted to tell people – to tell everyone in my midst – to stop what they were doing because the Angels were here and there was no need for them to do anything. Surely they knew there was nothing my friends and fellow students could do for the people stuck under the coach. Four of our group of people died that day including three fellow students and a friend of mine who sat behind me in the coach.

I endured three hairline fractures in my lower back. I refused the offer of an ambulance; I felt that others needed it more than me. I didn't think that I could accept assistance as all my life until that time I had not been good at accepting help. In fact, I preferred to draw back and put others before myself. I made a mistake that day. My shortsighted decision meant a longer road to physical recovery but I was young and healed nonetheless.

Looking back on this tragedy in the Yorkshire Dales, I consider a verse from the holy writings of *Kohelet* (Ecclesiastes 3:1–8) printed below.

For all of the trials and tribulations I endured that day and thereafter, I am deeply grateful I survived. I am deeply grateful for my life. In His infinite kindness God decided on that day I was not to die. I am forever grateful for His mercy.

I quote this verse in the memory of the dearly departed souls who ascended to Heaven that day. May they rest in peace:

To everything there is a season, and a time to every purpose
    under the heaven:
A time to be born, and a time to die;

A time to plant, and a time to pluck up that which is planted;

A time to kill, and a time to heal;

A time to break down, and a time to build up;

A time to weep, and a time to laugh;

A time to mourn, and a time to dance;

A time to cast away stones, and a time to gather stones together;

A time to embrace, and a time to refrain from embracing;

A time to seek, and a time to lose;

A time to keep, and a time to cast away;

A time to rend, and a time to sew;

A time to keep silence, and a time to speak;

A time to love, and a time to hate;

A time for war, and a time for peace.

Kohelet (Ecclesiastes 3:1–8)[1]

Chapter Three

In the midsummer of 1980, I am still a student at the University of Hull; it is the holidays. I have a temporary job. I work at the Harrods Food Halls in Knightsbridge, Central London. The Harrods Food Halls are world famous as is the store itself; it is a crème de crème department store in a high-class area of the capital city. Famous people who shop at Harrods mingle among international visitors who 'must visit' and also shop alongside regulars who regard Harrods as their 'local shop'.

I work on the delicatessen counter, selling various pâtés and French savories. My customers were very kind to me; polite and respectful. I am very slim, and at this time my hair is bobbed and my natural bright auburn red; everyone makes a fuss of me. I am in my element. I simply adore being surrounded by such glamour and plenty. The Harrods Food Halls are beautifully designed and the ambiance is something like a fairy tale to me, a girl from a humble home in Essex. There are shiny black and white tiles on the floor. Everywhere I look I see mirrors and glass and everything is pristine. There is no sense of lack in my midst. Harrods is like a King's Palace.

The bright lights of the Harrods Food Halls illuminate the focused concentration of the customers seeking 'manna in a temple of delight': in the form of Bulgarian caviar that costs more for a small tub than we at home had to live on for a week; in the perfectly sculptured forms of the luscious fruit; plump black grapes; varieties of shiny red and green apples; perfectly smooth oranges. Rare exotic flowers flown in from across the world cast heavenly fragrances that send me into ecstasy as I busily pass them, stroking the soft petals in wonder. Then there is under-lying all of these extravagances the combined smell of many other different foods including the dull, metallic smell of raw meats; and then there are the fresh fish counters and beyond the ready-made food to go and the places to sit and eat. The Harrods Food Halls go on and on.

But best and most wondrously of all there are plenty of gleanings. I am able to take home carrier bags of leftover food that would otherwise be thrown away; my mother and brothers anticipate my return home every night. By this time my father is no longer living with us. Every night we eat like Kings and Queens. I feel like the 'chosen one': I can now provide something for my family with ease. Most miraculously of all, in these days we had more than enough to eat.

The Harrods Food Halls at this time represented a place of abundance and safety. I loved working there. I felt happy, why shouldn't I be? I was twenty years old; I had a boyfriend and was re-sourced by my holiday pay and leftover food. For the first time in my life I was released from worry about how to make ends meet and if I would have enough to eat – and my family. Every day seemed like a dream until one day I was forced to shift my perspective into a different direction and remember whom I truly was.

I turn from serving a customer and suddenly I feel a chill going through my body. Unexpectedly, I am assailed with waves of thoughts that are totally alien to me. In that moment, I feel that I am absolutely nothing; my conscience is telling me I am unworthy. I am afraid; I feel like I am going to faint. I feel like life is absolutely pointless. I am drained of all energy and purpose.

Beside me stands a middle-aged man in a white chef's hat; he comes into focus. It is the manager of the section of the Food Halls where I have been assigned. I know who he is; he is an educated and decent man; a fair manager. But I imagine that his career aspirations were originally higher than where he has ended up. All of a sudden, without a warning he begins to speak to me in a very personal way, from his heart, from a place of deep emotion. He talks of his private inner turmoil: his fears; his disappointments; his concerns; his troubles. I listen but all the while I know what he is going to say next; there is a dictation of his 'speech' being 'fed' to me from somewhere and I can hear it in my head. All the while this complete stranger who was my manager talked to me about his deepest most personal feelings I know what he is going to say; I can hear his words before he says them.

All of the activity around us becomes distant. We are in a small and concentrated bubble; for the duration of this Divinely ordained conversational experience I feel in complete spiritual union with this man; I feel I am 'holding' him energetically as he gives me his story. From a place of anguish and despair he told me that he woke up feeling a sense of hopelessness and lack of worth and that at this moment he feels dreadful. His voice is articulate; he is not facing me. I stand beside him; he talks into the space before us both.

When he first began to talk I had immense feelings of worthlessness but as the man continued to talk these feelings of my own dissipated. Startled, I realized that I had telepathically picked up on my manager's thoughts and heard the musings of his soul without him having to say one word out loud to me. I could almost have transcribed them for him before he uttered one word to me.

Unschooled as I was at the time of this psychic phenomena, initially I had no means of discerning between the two of us which thoughts were mine and which were his. But as he continued to talk I realized that what he was saying I was able to hear before him, and what I had felt before he spoke was not directly linked to how I personally felt about myself. Regardless, I could not believe what was happening to me; it was the most odd and frightening experience I had felt in my life.

All I could do when I was in this experience was stand beside my manager and listen very deeply from a place of great stillness and compassion; I felt so very empathic to his plight. When he stopped talking, without any dialogue between us, words of comfort came unbidden out of me. I told him that far from being worthless he was a decent and kind person; these were immensely valuable traits. My positive reflection and instinctive empathetic healing moved him through and out of his despair. The negativity dispersed. The busy world of Harrods came rushing in. The cost of the healing had been to take his pain as my own. We turned back to our work and never spoke between ourselves of what had happened.

Chapter Four

Aged twenty-two, I have completed my BA Honors Degree. The study of Sociology has influenced me and I am leaning towards the Socialist side of my family. I advocate, to whoever listens to me, that "it was only through human endeavor we could progress mankind by means of the application of the rational thought and the redistribution of wealth." I am very sure of myself. As far as I am concerned religion and spirituality are methods used to control the masses; I consider the concept of 'Chi' or Energy Force (its translation in Japanese) a complete joke, a delusion.

Unfortunately, my concern at the problems in the world is overtaken by my own practical considerations. Now that I had left university I didn't know where I should live. I couldn't go back home. Not only has my younger brother now moved into my bedroom, I also feel that it would be a retrogressive step. I am unclear what I want to do with my life. I am torn. On the one hand I am drawn to the marble abundance of the Harrods Food Halls. I came from an upbringing of poverty; a family living with the daily fear we might not eat at the next mealtime among other lacks. My mother in particular has taught me that I must care for everyone. This is the person I was becoming: an empathic soul; a giving, thoughtful person who serves others. I am not sure what to do: should I take a corporate job and work for money or enter community service and do acts of kindness all day and be paid for putting the needs of others first? I want to do both; I want both worlds and the benefits of both jobs. But I can't see how to make my needs for both transfer into a working reality. I put my conflict and dilemma to one side and opt for a gap year to consider my options and open up the possibilities. Maybe I should work abroad, look at new ways to give to the world and earn a salary. I go beyond the limitations of my upbringing and myself and buy the cheapest ticket I can find and head to the Middle East. I travel to Israel. I volunteer on a secular kibbutz in Galilee, in the north of Israel. I naively assume travel and living a simple communal life with my international brethren would afford me answers to all the questions spinning around my head, heart and soul. I am young and extremely opinionated; I think that I know it all. Obviously, I am a very poor listener. I know exactly what world leaders need to do to make the world a better place.

My kibbutz experience includes a visit to Jerusalem. Even I, possibly at that time in my life the most spiritually and religiously resistant being on planet Earth, can't help noticing that in Jerusalem the air was different: that something magical was happening in my midst; that in the atmosphere there was a palatable feeling of Holiness. It is so prevalent I feel the air pulsing; everywhere I look I can see a vibrant light around people and particular objects and places.

As if compelled, I immediately leave the kibbutz in the north of Israel to go the capital Jerusalem. I stay with a family, working to earn my room and board. I abandon my nonsensical attitude and start to notice and listen more carefully to what is going on around me; I am so inspired by this eternal light I begin to draw and paint and can't stop. What is really odd is that every one of my paintings has a glowing halo around the people and trees, for that is what I see and that is what I paint.

I decide that I am going to earn my living by being an artist. I attend art classes run by Jerusalem artist David Rakia. I find that all I want to do is to follow the glow that was pulling me like a magnetic force around the city of Jerusalem. It was like the Silver Rope from my childhood had reappeared but this time it was in the guise of a golden glowing light on my path every day. Everywhere I looked there was an abundance of spiritual richness. Unlike the Harrods Food Halls this was not material richness; it was a spiritual wealth. I am intensely aware of universality; often feeling so ecstatic by the many examples that Jerusalem provided of this that I am dizzy, joyful and tearful at the oddest moments, so powerful and affecting is the source of light and what it illuminates for me.

To get by while I am in training to be an artist I find part-time jobs; housekeeping and babysitting for families near where I room and board. In this way I became integrated in Jerusalem life. I also take a volunteer job at The British School of Archaeology; for three months I work on excavation sites that are commonplace around Jerusalem and Israel.

One day, our crew dug out a cave outside of the city of Jerusalem in the French Hill district, near to the route to the Dead Sea in the Negev, the desert region in the south of Israel. It was like a child's version of a cave, maybe 6 foot wide and 6 foot high. The cave had been turned into a very simple tomb, a resting place for someone who had died in the community. It was completely filled up with mud. It took all day to carefully sift this mud out. By mid-afternoon it was clear this site had been desecrated during a robbery. The marble sarcophagus and its contents lay shattered in several pieces on the floor; remains of bones were present.

As we continued to clear away the unwanted mass a niche was uncovered in the stone entranceway to the tomb: a tiny ledge; a shelf where it was clear an oil lamp had been placed. On the wall beside the ledge was the dark outline of the flicker of a candle flame. Perhaps a family member had visited the tomb and rested an oil lamp on the ledge.

I stood and looked at this testimony of attendance and respect, service and honor. From where I stood on the hill I had a clear view of the Dead Sea glimmering in the distance. For a moment, I felt at one with my surroundings. We had uncovered evidence of how a human being is buried and honored. The tiny ledge in this tomb with its dark outline of a flame from an oil lamp had touched me deeply. For me, this mark of visitation, this remnant of a visit to someone's burial site, represented life after death; triumph of good over the evil act of desecration by the grave robbers.

I imagined the flame of the oil lamp that had been rested on the tiny shelf. A flame is a symbol of eternal life. When I see a flame, I think of the world beyond the material; beyond the here and now. A candle flame has a transcendental effect on me; it inspires in me spiritual feelings and calm follows. I looked from the dark outline of the flame to the shattered marble sarcophagus and decided then and there what to do. I must return home to my mother, to my family and do the right thing. I could no longer stay away from home putting off making a decision. I had to go back; mine was not to be a path of digging up a deceased person's past, or of capturing moments in time by painting, although I have the deepest love of art and still retain a respect for archeology. I saw very clearly that I did not want to be involved in making things. Of the two remnants left in the cave, the marble sarcophagus and the shadow of the flame of the oil lamp, it was the flame that had endured as tangible evidence that it was showing up that counted; that the care and the attention to human life in this world and beyond is what mattered to me.

I realized then, as I know now, there was no real dilemma; there was no dichotomy. Whatever I decided to do would not change the fact I was a compassionate person; that I wanted to do something with my life which would impact positively on people and the world. That I love people and I want to work with people. The dark shadow of that flame outline in that cave in Jerusalem showed me that tiny individual acts of kindness endure, that loves endures. And I wanted to dedicate my life to acts of kindness for the sake of the love of humanity. This I felt was an honorable way to live my life.

I worked my fare back to London as soon as I could. I returned home to my mother; we moved the bedrooms around to make room for me in the busy house with three younger brothers now aged 14 to 18. There was a place for me until I found work and could afford to rent my own apartment. I chose to work in social housing in local government. It was a good choice. I learned to serve the community of my birth and upbringing. I had a secure income. I felt secure in my work and I earned a living, and I should have been contented.

I have thought about our discovery at the tomb in the French Hill for more than thirty years. As time has passed, and I have gained more knowledge about life and living, I have come to realize even more from reading and personal experience with end-of-life, and talking to my personal Angel, clients and Spiritual teachers, that although the body, the container of the soul, is not enduring, it is only love, like the flicker of the flame retained on a wall in the tomb in the French Hill, that is truly long-lasting. As we go about our days performing our acts of kindness and devotion to our family, friends, our lovers, colleagues and even strangers, our thoughtfulness has a tangible presence as well as eternal ramifications. The light of our soul is eternal; that our soul continues on forever when we no longer have use for our bodies. Memories of those in this world are kindled by the love they received from those they have lost; what we leave behind when we go to the next world is the love in the hearts of those we shared our love with.

Like a fragrance, a soul cannot be held. Yes, it is part of us, it flows through us, it is us – the life force of our being, the personality that defines us – but our soul is not a tangible entity; we cannot hope to hold onto our soul forever. When we are with someone who passes away, when we experience the end-of-life stage with someone we know, we may sit by their bedside and talk to them; experience their soul in their personality; enjoy our final moments with the uniqueness of who they are. Yet when they are gone, their soul has departed. There lies before us a shell, the human form, the material body of the person; and contained within that physical form everything that person needed to function on a material level, their heart that like a miracle does not stop beating for all of their days, their organs, their blood, for example. But their soul, the uniqueness of their self, their personality, their unique and distinctive life force, is not present; it has ascended. It no longer exists in material terms, only in memory and only in the Spirit.

When the soul of a human being finally leaves this world it begins a new journey with a new purpose. It begins to travel between two worlds serving its Creator in the Upper Realms and returning to the Lower Realms to comfort and guide us. Therefore the body, the place the soul once rested and lived, has no use to them or us anymore, which is why it has to be given respect and laid to rest accordingly.

On that day in Jerusalem, in the French Hill at the tomb, there were no heavenly Angels present that I saw or heard; people had made the shadow of the flame. Writing this now I am filled with gratitude for that dark shadow of the flame on that cave wall, for that sign of remembrance from people who visited the cave was a sign for me. It sent me on my way. It sent me towards my true vocation, my true calling.

Chapter Five

It is September 1989. I am standing in a small rather scruffy corner office on the fourth floor of a government office building in North London. The carpet is stained; the walls are covered with various instructions and peeling tape. I am now working in local government as a Social Housing Manager. I look out of the window of my office wondering what I am doing here in this city with grey skies. I let my eyes wander over the rooftops of the local area; rooftops always remind me of my childhood but this time I cannot see the rooftops of my grandparents' homes. That was a long time ago. Now I am an adult trying to make a go of life but things are rather dull and I do not feel beloved to anyone including myself; in fact I am rather at odds with myself. Although I am passionate about my work I also find it hard at times because I miss being free.

Abruptly, I feel a sense of being hemmed in and feel claustrophobic as if I have no room to breathe. There is a pressure on my body. I feel like I am in a crowded room; it feels as if many souls are pressing themselves against me. I turn and look across the hallway into the office of a colleague, a woman I work with; I know her sister Ann.*

Suddenly I grow still and alert. I hear the voice of what I then termed "my intuition". It tells me: "Ann is pregnant, she doesn't know it yet, she is going to have a baby girl." I wander out of my office to my colleague's office across the way and (with scant regard for confidentiality) matter-of-factly announce to Ann's sister: "Ann is pregnant. She doesn't know yet. It's a girl." My colleague looked at me and nodded. Nothing more was said; I went back to my work.

Nine months later, on returning home to the apartment where I now lived with my husband, he said to me:

"Ann has had her baby. It's a boy. His name is Robin."

I replied: "No, that is not right, she is having a girl."

Later that day, I heard that my colleague's sister Ann had called her new baby daughter Robyn. When my husband confirmed this fact I smiled. My spiritual gift had reestablished itself in my life. Renewed hope and feelings of untapped possibilities surged through my days and nights. But let me go back a few years and tell you about the time my husband and I first met.

*Name changed to protect privacy.

Chapter Six

I have a core value that if something becomes coercive then it loses its authority. In my mind all of our transactions should be of equal benefit to each party: that whenever possible there should be a give and a take between people; respect; an invitation rather than a must.

In this book that tells the story of my own personal relationship with my own Personal Angel I recount that I chose to become Jewish. I want to make it very clear at this juncture of my story that this was my personal choice. I am not advocating any religion or choice in this book; whatever the reader takes from my story so be it. This part of my story is just that: a chapter in my life that forms a backdrop to the journey that I took to embrace my spirituality and come to know my own Personal Angel.

I want to preface this chapter with the following note of consideration: You will come to notice as you read this book that if I talk of other religions it is only in context to the story I wish to tell; this is my policy. I leave religion to the experts and those that are committed to their own religious way of life. I do not profess to be an expert on religion, only on spiritual matters. In 1981, I met my future husband. When he asked me to marry him I agreed to convert to his religion of birth, Judaism. I undertook the process to become a Reform Jew; it took two years.

It was an easy decision for me to become a Jewish woman; I had been inspired long ago by the kindness and the value system of my first boyfriend Adam's family. My affinity to Judaism had been strengthened during my visit to Israel a year earlier. I felt ready to take on this religious obligation and responsibility. I wanted a home of my own and I wanted our life together to have a foundation of spiritual value and faith. The two-year education I received in preparation for my conversion prepared me well for my new future with my husband. It gave me the self-assurance to become a wife; and when I was blessed with children I felt able to undertake my duty from an informed place with the appropriate outlook, with the love and support of my future husband.

Blessedly, I did not face a lot of resistance from my own family for my choice to follow the ways of my new husband's faith. My family was a mixed bunch: Socialists on my mother's side and Baptist Christians on my father's side. I was sent to Sunday School from the age of five. Sometime after I understood what was happening at Sunday School I came home and announced to my family: "I believe in God but I do not believe in Jesus." This elicited laughter from one and all except from my Aunt Gill who is a committed Christian; she was shocked.

The laughter that accompanied my viewpoint on Jesus did not affect my long-term vision at this tender, vulnerable age. I chose not to become affiliated to a church or any particular religious doctrine. Yet, the kindness, hospitality and unconditional acceptance I received during the four years I was a guest in the home of that first boyfriend who was Jewish was a deciding factor in me choosing to embrace Judaism as a way of life. A Jewish way of life embedded in order and discipline, and adherence to laws and ethics. Gradually, I learned the Jewish approach to life and living would be a good investment for my future and that of my future children.

My fiancé Steven was very supportive during the two-year preparation for my formal Jewish conversion interview and exam. I had a lot to learn and I knew it would take a lifetime to gain true faith and trust in this new religion; I was committed and was grateful for this wonderful new opportunity. I looked forward to becoming his wife. During the Jewish Reform conversion process we attended educational classes together at The Settlement Reform Synagogue in the East End of London. For this is the law in the United Kingdom: if you want to become a Reform Jew your fiancé, even if he is a Jew by birth, which takes its line of birthright through the mother, has to attend classes with you. On the completion of my two years of study before I had my final official interview with the certifying Reform Rabbis, I traveled four hours by car to Cardiff in Wales to undertake the final stage of my Reform conversation process. In a utilitarian municipal building I undertook immersion in a *Mikvah*, which is the custom by Jewish Law. A *Mikvah* is a pool of pure rainwater. I had to submerge in the water after saying a series of prayers in Hebrew. The room where I was to follow this procedure was lit from natural light; the specifically sized pool of water is big enough to stand in and turn around. There is preparation before immersing which one does in private and a female attendant oversees the immersion to certify it is kosher by Jewish Law.

With trepidation and gratitude, I immersed my full body in the water. The water was slightly warm; it was a very comforting experience, perhaps a bit like returning to the birth sac before one is born. Under the water, I remember feeling a rush of happiness at fulfilling this holy commandment; I felt a great sense of appreciation to my fiancé for asking me to marry him. As I rose out of the water a strange occurrence happened. The unadorned room that housed the *Mikvah* pool where the light had been natural was now filled with a golden light so bright and beautiful that I inhaled a breath of awe and shock. The attendant was visibly moved also. "What is going on?" she said.

I was not sure, but one thing I did know. A holy Angel was visiting me; I could feel her energy and I could see her light. I felt supported at this auspicious time and I think that it was the most beautiful experience of my life until that time.

Later that day, I was interviewed by a Board of Reform Rabbis who are appointed to officially grant conversion status. That day I became a Reform Jew. Even though my husband and I were blessed to be married for only twenty-seven years we still consider ourselves to be friends. I cannot tell you why we are no longer married; that is personal. But I can tell you that our time together was special and that we have no regrets; and today we have a peaceful arrangement, and together in our own way we support and raise our sons.

But I am rushing ahead a little now so I will tell you of a few more experiences that inspired and prompted me in 2010 to change my life, to work as an Angel Reader, Energy Healer and Intuitive Coach.

Chapter Seven

After we had been married for two years, in October 1990 my husband and I were in a state of intense grief; we had lost our first child through a miscarriage. We were devastated. I blamed myself because I had felt the soul of the baby at the moment of conception and was convinced that she had decided not to incarnate because of my bad temper; that due to this character trait I was constantly trying to refine God did not deem me fit to be a mother. I was racked with pain and had no belief that I would ever conceive again.

After the miscarriage we took a respite; we left hectic London for a weekend away in a little quiet village in Crewkerne, Somerset, in the South West of England. When we arrived I was in a very sad state, feeling depressed and crying a lot. We decided to go for a stroll. While we were browsing at books in a secondhand bookshop in town, a poetry book literally threw itself off the top shelf, hit me on the head and landed on the floor at my feet. After gathering my wits about me, I bent down and picked up the book. The pages open in the book revealed a poem about a fair-haired and beautiful baby boy.

As I recall this story I feel a great rush of emotion; I can so easily recall the accompanying relief and grace that I felt when I read this poem. I am convinced now that it was my personal Angel speaking to me through the poem, reassuring me that everything was going to be all right. And so it was.

Over the next nine years we were blessed with two beautiful sons. Our eldest son Joshua, born in 1991, was a lovely baby at birth. The moment that he was born he was handed to me and before I made any movement towards him, his hand tenderly touched my face. Joshua had the fair hair mentioned in the poem. In an incredibly busy hospital (the Royal Free Hospital in Hampstead, London) there were staff coming into the ward just to look at him because they had heard that an exceptionally beautiful baby had been born. (Apologies, Josh, for telling this story.) My second son Zachary, born in 1999, was also a beautiful baby, weighing 10.5lbs, the same weight as the twins being born in the next room combined. I always tell Zachary he weighed this much because he is as fantastic as two people in one.

Chapter Eight

In December 2003, I believe that I first encountered Archangel Raphael; I know this now because today in 2015 I am a healer. I think He may have assisted me at other times and I was unaware it was Him; it was only after I undertook intensive training that I gained knowledge of the Archangels and how to recognize them.

When Zachary was aged three years old, I suffered the loss of a paternal uncle who was like a father to me. I had a father but this uncle pretty much took on the role of looking after me. My biological father was not capable of undertaking his duties; Uncle Vic took over helping my mother. Due to a dispute over my Uncle Vic's last will and testament, my immediate family disowned me; they could not come to terms with the fact my uncle left me his estate as a gift.

Uncle Vic died around the time my husband was diagnosed with the illness lupus, a nasty and insidious disease. During this time period from when Uncle Vic died and my husband's diagnosis – a matter of six months – I was incapacitated and overwhelmed with grief. But like most women in these circum-stances with two young sons, who needed me, and a husband seriously ill, who also needed me, I had no choice but to carry on.

One winter day, after I took Zachary to nursery, I drove home through Walnut Tree in Milton Keynes, down a quiet suburban road, past houses and gardens. It was snowing and the day was very bright. The radio in the car was turned off but suddenly the car was full of the sound of singing. It was a rendition of the carol *Silent Night*. It was so beautiful that as I am writing it now twelve years later, I am moved to tears. I stopped the car and walked around it trying to find the source of the music.

There was no music outside but still music coming from everywhere in my midst. The street was so quiet I could hear my own breathing. There was not a person in sight. Everywhere was white and I could not work out where the sound of this music was coming from. How could this be happening? I turned off the car engine, but still the music was there. I turned the radio on and then off again and still the music continued. I checked the CD but it was empty. The music continued soaring and filling my heart with a mixture of joy, grief and gratitude. I now believe that I was hearing an Angelic choir (my inner knowing says this music was brought to me by Archangel Raphael). The choir was singing to give me strength and courage to manage the loss of my beloved uncle and the challenge of estrangement from my family.

Chapter Nine

Some of my friends say that this following story is evidence of good luck rather than Angelic intervention. However, I think otherwise.

By 2009 my relationship with my husband was growing difficult and I decided to make matters worse by going on a 'radical manifestation' cruise in the Caribbean run by Colin Tipping.[2] Looking back it was inconsiderate of me as my husband was just recovering from an illness. He had just supported me through the Bi-Aura[3] energy training that I will tell you about in the section that follows, 'Transition'; he would never have dreamt of going on a holiday on his own without our sons Josh and Zachary. But to me, at that time, being on my 'spiritual journey' really meant breaking out of domesticity, which often bored me, and doing what I wanted regardless of the cost. As far as I was concerned I was actually 'working'. So despite opposition I went.

This story has nothing to do with the cruise, which was amazing. However, at the end of the seven days I was feeling quite guilty, anxious to come home, especially wanting to get back to Zachary who was only eight years old at the time. The plan was to take a flight from Florida to Dallas, then home to Heathrow. But as we landed in Dallas we were informed by loudspeaker that the flight to Heathrow was cancelled. The loudspeaker continued to tell us that there was a hope of getting back because there was a BA flight leaving shortly and that had 160 spare places, and that this flight could take some of the 200 passengers whose flight was cancelled.

Not only were all of my fellow passengers already in line for the next plane; they were all in survival mode with equally compelling reasons to have a seat on that plane and fighting their corner. I was not in survival mode because I was blissed out at the end of the course: very open; very engrossed in my new metaphysical book. I went to look at the queue and walked around it assessing whether or not I could slip in (I told you that I was selfish in those days). There was absolutely no chance whatsoever. So I calmly walked to the back of the queue; continued to read my book on radical manifestation; visualized myself on the flight and prayed.

When I as the last person in line finally arrived at the flight check-in desk, I looked the stewardess in the eye and said, "I need you to help me, I must get home," to which she, with her eyes filled with compassion replied, "I am sorry, Madam, but there are no places."

I replied, "Please just check. I have a feeling that there is a place." She shook her head and because I was insistent checked her computer. Then she was in disbelief, "I can't believe it! A place has become available! Take this ticket and run." I seized the ticket and ran like the wind. I got on the plane and was arrogant enough to complain that I did not also obtain an upgrade.

However, getting home on time did not save my marriage; my ex-husband told me recently that as far as he was concerned the fact that I had been on the cruise was 'the final straw'. But to this day I will never forget how pleased I was to see Zachary and Josh again. And despite what some friends say, I know that a seat on a fully-booked flight didn't arrive out of thin air. I was only lucky in that my Angel was working her magic for me. Again!

Chapter Ten

In May 2010 a new government was elected in the UK. Almost immediately my livelihood began to fall away. Most crucially a large piece of work that I had been promised failed to materialize. The withdrawal of funds in one local government department meant the end of the line for me. I had had no foresight that this would happen. I was totally unprepared and frozen into a state of panic. Even if Angels wanted to help me I was not about to be able to hear them through channeling. I was a rabbit caught in the headlights. Usually I was proactive. Now I was immobile. From May until July I had no idea of what I should do.

On the night of 17th July 2010, I was sitting with Kim, a friend of mine. We were discussing work prospects; I needed to improve my financial situation and I had no idea how I was going to do that. My situation felt very stark indeed. By now I was divorced and the consultancy business into which I had put all my resources was no longer functioning.

Kim is a good listener. I told her all my concerns and the bottom line, but we came up with no new ideas. I went to sleep that night none-the-wiser but my friend's empathy made an impression on me.

Later that same night, I dreamt that I was sitting with my friend Kim. There was a large glass, brightly-colored jukebox on the floor in front of us. Kim pointed to a song-card on the front of the jukebox: "You could play that one," she said to me. I then admired the jukebox. In the dream Kim told me that she bought it from a company called Funky Monkey, on the Internet. By the way it wasn't cheap, it cost £960!

The next morning I searched online for Funky Monkey. This was my first hit. http://www.funkymonkey.com/.[4] The site is still up but this entry that I speak of here has been taken down; I don't know why but it is not there now. On that day though, you could access a selection of songs and poems including the sweet composition Kim suggested I play in the dream from the night before. The song began: "There is this need in me to make something that matters and speaks to me, something that may make things a little bit better for everyone. When you are feeling discouraged you can come here and find one more little island of positive intention and belief."

The site was trademarked to KIN – so it was clever that the Angel used my friend KIM to direct me to it. Not only that but the site was designed and managed by a person who called himself or herself Michel Angel. The layers of cleverness went deeper. I clicked on the navigational tool under the section labeled 'breath' and there was a picture of an Angel and under the picture was a message for me which said: "Follow your dreams and don't doubt." This was a message that was much needed as my world of local government and consultancy was fast slipping away, which had brought me to confusion and despair. This dream was a much-needed dream.

How many Internet sites are there in the world? Millions – I know. But that day I looked at only one; one that added to my belief system that Angels talk to me in dreams and when I am awake.

Considering all of the above I hope that you will be able to understand why I welcomed this dream. It is due to the extreme dislocation that I have experienced in my life through unasked for change that I have always taken dream messages of this sort seriously and been comforted by them. Here the Archangel Mikel helped me in my everyday life. It's not a majorly dramatic episode. I wasn't rescued from a burning building, but because I faced a major change in my circumstances the verification comforted, held me and gave me the confidence to set off in a new direction.

For all of my adult life I had explored the spiritual world as a hobby – even training as a healer – but it was a hobby that I kept quiet about. I kept the two spheres separate, seeing them as distinct as oil and water. So from my perspective this dream was a much-needed dream. Probably from the perspective of my Angels and Guides also. My lack of responsiveness to my situation was putting me in danger. It was time to let go of the past. I had to get moving and I had to get moving fast. So I did. I decided to cross the Bridge from earning my way in the Material world to work in the Spiritual world as a Healer. In the next section you will see how the healing evolved into Angel Channeling and the Angel Channeling evolved into Intuitive Coaching. It was quite a journey.

Part Two
Transition

And he began to see the truth, that Ged had neither lost nor won but, naming the shadow of his death with his own name, had made himself whole; a man; who, knowing his whole true self, cannot be used or possessed by any power other than himself, and whose life therefore is lived for life's sake and never in the service of ruin, or pain, or hatred, or the dark. In the creation of Ea which is the oldest song, it is said, "only in silence the word, only in dark the light, only in dying life; bright the hawk's flight on the empty sky."

"The Open Sea", page 166, *The Earthsea Quartet* by Ursula Le Guin (Penguin, 1993)

Chapter One

It took until I was fifty to fully step into my spirituality and believe in the fact that (like all of us to one degree or another) I have a power to facilitate healing and that I have a skill and expertise which sometimes assists people in being 'fully on the Earth'. I have realized that although not everyone is comfortable with the fact (may sometimes be startled) I do channel an energy that I perceive to be an Angel. That it's OK and I am not 'bonkers' to be on a 'spiritual path', or if I am a 'little bit left of center' that's OK. However, I don't have to flag it up every time; I can just be with it. In short it has taken me more than thirty years to stop apologizing for and denying who I am and to be content in my skin.

It wasn't that I had any desire to be an alternative healer that led me to Bi-Aura therapy: it was a gut reaction. I am empathetic. Often friends would come and sit with me and tell me their story; I would give some instinctive but rough and ready untrained healing, e.g. heart energy and hands on shoulders; they would leave energized and happy; I would retire to bed for a few days to recover. The reason that the healing impacted upon me so strongly was that I had no concept of energy hygiene, and was using my own limited resources rather than the unlimited resources of the universe to reenergize and heal.

I was attracted to Bi-Aura because I read about it in a newspaper and the article 'leapt up' at me. Although I was skeptical about new age philosophy, once I had started to see auras in Jerusalem I came back to England open enough to attend Gill Edwards' Living Magically course. The only reason that I countenanced the course was that I perceived Gill as properly qualified and non-wacky because she was recognized in the 'real world', e.g. a trained clinical psychotherapist.

Gill taught me to 'live magically' by listening to my inner

wisdom and intuition, and having the courage to follow my gut instinct. Gill Edwards died young; she lived 24 May 1956–19 November 2011. She packed more into her lifetime than most people do in several lifetimes, and I am indebted to all that she taught me, and still use her books and recommend them.

Although Gill was teaching us (her group over a year) to have the courage to 'live magically' and create 'Heaven here on Earth' and could have acted like a 'guru', she was very down to earth and non-judgmental. When I arrived at her first workshop I was carrying an extremely large drawing pad – about three feet by two and a half feet because her instructions were **"bring a large notebook"**; I am extremely literal and did exactly as asked. I was also very late, so I when I walked into a room full of 'spiritual' people, each writing in an appropriate e.g. normal-sized notebook, I was hugely embarrassed by my enormous 'notebook'. But Gill didn't make me feel bad; I was welcomed in, no one disparaged the drawing pad. In fact a participant congratulated me because I was 'so out there' and expressive. When I look back at this episode I think that it's very funny and my then husband Steven found it hilarious. The moral is that when you are on your spiritual path, as long as you are not harming anyone you can more or less get away with anything if you keep your nerve.

So lesson number one on my 'spiritual path' was to learn to laugh at my own absurdity. Not a bad lesson at all! Anyway I am digressing – by a 'leaping up' or a gut reaction I mean a flash of intuition, or a shining around something. When this happens it's worth sitting up and paying attention. If you decide to embark on or already are on a 'spiritual' path this resonance is and will be one of your best friends; it will aid you in separating the authentic from the inauthentic. The esoteric world is open to a lot of interpretation. Many people will tell you many things. Some may be useful, some may be healing; but some may be judgmental and damaging or inappropriate, or just their projection.

The inner knowing in and flashing up and shining that accompanied the Bi-Aura article was worth following because the Bi-Aura course was exactly right for me especially as it led me to being able to see and be able to integrate my Angel.

In the summer of 2008, I was at the dentist waiting to be seen for my six-monthly check-up. I picked up a tabloid newspaper, one that I would not normally buy. It had an article about Bi-Aura Energy Healing.[1] The article became luminous and started to shine at me. I was transfixed to learn in a mainstream newspaper that people were experiencing healing through energy work. I read on to learn that Bi-Aura Energy Healing is a noninvasive energy technique that works by clearing and rebalancing Chakras through using Earth and cosmic energy to allow the body to heal itself.

The resonance was so strong and I was so interested that I applied immediately to the Bi-Aura Foundation for a place on their course to train and become a certified Bi-Aura Healer. I funded it through my consultancy work and ran it alongside my mainstream work. The training took place at Regent College, London, throughout 2008–2009. The curriculum included practical training of healing techniques and theory, both of which were assessed by examination. Once the examinations were successfully over not only was I qualified as a Bi-Aura Healer, I could also apply for insurance to cover me as a practitioner. That was all well and good, but the Bi-Aura training brought along access to something extra and that something extra was a personal Angel who is named Celestial Bell (CB for short).

I think that it is fair to say that for a long time I made it difficult for my personal Angel to reach me; I resisted her messages. I was also initially quite overwhelmed by her presence in my life. But she was persistent. And now I am glad she was!

When I was discussing the idea to write this book with my

twenty-something son Josh, he remembered that when he was eight years old I told him that I had dream in which he had opened the door and came to get me saying: "Your Angel is here, please come and talk to her." Within my dream, all those years ago, I had refused to see her. Years ago, I was still refusing to allow my Angel into my life; the idea of connecting with any spirit of any kind was utterly terrifying and to be avoided.

My attitude towards my Angel changed during one weekend on the Bi-Aura course. We were carrying out a guided meditation in which I saw myself as a small child. When I followed this visualization my Angel took me by surprise: I looked back and saw myself as a child surrounded by departed relatives standing around me in a protective circle, and over my head stood a huge Art Nouveau-inspired green Angel. I was both very afraid and astounded.

The tradition among Jewish scholars is that a person should not begin to study the Kabbalah, the most holy, mystical Jewish writings, until they are forty, the age that a person is mature enough to cope with the weight of such insights and knowledge. Witnessing and receiving messages from a spiritual being can be a frightening experience but with the right support a relationship and connection can be established and nurtured with 'The Other World' that is safe and productive. You really need to know yourself – your strengths and weaknesses – and be trained or guided appropriately when dealing with Angelic beings; this is my understanding and viewpoint today.

When I finally decided to recognize CB and begin a relationship with her it did take time to establish a rapport; it even took me a few months to find the courage to speak with her, even to be able to ask her name. When I talk of the National Gallery experience with CB that I mention on page 129, you are hearing about her in an assertive situation. CB was determined to get me inside that gallery and she did. She had something important to tell me; it goes without saying CB doesn't take no for an answer! But when I think about the beginning of our relationship, I can recall my personal Angel being very gentle with me. I think it has taken about seven years since our first interaction for me to have full confidence and faith in CB despite her astonishing accuracy, and the fact that she has helped me to help many people, giving hope, healing and grounding by assisting with healing and giving channeled messages pertinent to each person.

You are probably wondering how my personal Angel contacts me. Once I had seen her during the Bi-Aura meditation during a guided class in 2009, I started to feel her in my presence on a constant basis. Then I found that I could contact her at will through raising my vibration, a bit like tuning into a station on a radio by finding the right frequency. I bring myself within my head and reach up, and then listen inwardly to what she has to say. Usually I find it easiest if I write down what I hear, which also helps my clients as they then have something to take away with them.

When I eventually calmed down and started to listen to my personal Angel she told me that her name was Celestial Bell. I thought that this was hilarious and laughed but she sternly told me: "Celestial Bell is a very common name among Angels." Even now I think that this is the most ridiculous of names – but perhaps it's the right name for my Angel because I dislike hierarchies so much. I am determined to try not to come to my work as an Angel Channeler from a place of ego. If it had been a grand name or she was an Archangel there would have a real danger that I would have closed down altogether. I would have felt too intimated to talk to her and consider what she was prompting me to do, to become 'professional partners' so to speak. For I know the work I do as an Angel Channeler I cannot do without her.

A friend nicknamed Celestial Bell; CB for short and that is what I call her now. In China, there is a sacred mountain called

Celestial Bell. Metaphysical companies make and sell Celestial Bells which are used for 'Clearing', another form of energy healing; as one of my specialties now is Energetic Clearing this made sense to me. I am very grateful to some of my close friends who recognized, validated and believed in CB long before I did. I was often skeptical while they were often saying: "Wendy, look, what CB is saying and you are channeling is true."

It is largely because I learned how to communicate with CB that I set out on the journey of self-realization, which I describe in the following chapters. This was a journey that led to me being able to meet the father from whom I had long been estranged. Although that fact was the destination, the motive for starting the journey was different. I was determined to work on myself, to raise my energy vibration and become a purer vessel to receive her messages to pass on. I accept messages from CB to help others; that is my prime intention.

There is no place for ego in the work I do. I have to draw back or nullify myself to be a conduit for my Angel's communication from the higher realms to this world. But I had to learn how to receive from CB; I needed to prepare my 'vessel' – my mind, heart, soul and body – and learn how to live in the material and rational world at the same time as receiving Angelic intervention. Not an easy task! In Part One of this book, I tell you of the initial experiences that happened to me when I was largely unconscious of my psychic abilities and still inexperienced in spiritual channeling.

In Part Two, this section of the book, I have outlined a selection of the training and educational processes that I undertook, and some of the things that happened, which enabled me to be able to 'hear' and accept the guidance from my Angel more effectively; in so doing I truly believe in my own way I have been helpful to humankind, and in the process assisted in the vast task of helping to repair the world we live in.

Chapter Two

For many reasons, I found Bi-Aura Healing training a good investment for my future spiritual work.

The Bi-Aura Foundation is a registered charity. The training certified, ethical and professional. The one-year training program I undertook was accredited with a qualification equivalent to an NVQ 4, which enables practitioners to become insured. I attended eight residential weekends in London. The teaching standards were excellent; the post-training supportive. Generously the Bi-Aura Foundation provides ongoing support once training is complete, its website lists practitioners, continuation training is offered.

Bi-Aura Healing training was good value for money. The process felt transparent; the trainers maintained a professional attitude; they were dedicated and caring which helped me to feel safe and supported as I charted this unfamiliar yet extraordinary world of Energy Healing.

The greatest benefit of this training program was that during one of my early meditation sessions I met and verified my own personal Angel CB; until this time she had tried to connect with me but I had been resistant. Within the framework of Bi-Aura Healing I was able to recognize my mystic and psychic abilities and realize CB's presence in my life was a foreshown conclusion; if I wanted to work as a Spiritual Guide I needed to accept the guidance of my own Spiritual Mentor, Celestial Bell, and I did with great joy – finally.

I want to make it very clear at this juncture in my story the Bi-Aura Healing course was not designed as a course in Angel Channeling. It just so happened that while I was undertaking Bi-Aura Healing training I had an encounter with my own personal Angel. I did not tell anyone this happened, I did not speak about CB to anyone on this course; I kept quiet about her and my acceptance of her commitment to me. But from the circumstances that transpired after we forged our relationship, it was clear to me that my fellow students on the course became aware of a change in me and were conscious of an energy field around me, which was CB. For example, in April 2010 her presence was recognized while I was being tested in my Bi-Aura Healing practical examination. Just the week before I had been told that I might fail the practical examination because – although "I definitely had the juice", i.e. was a strong healer – I habitually dream and forget to pay attention to detail. Bi-Aura Healing is carried out by specific hand movements and specific intent, which I often bypassed and disregarded in favor of my own methodology. Anyway my instructors were cross with me, wanting me to adhere strictly to the course methodology.

There was one technique that I found especially difficult; it involves drawing down and flushing both cosmic and Earth energy through a person. I couldn't get it right. Whenever I tried to undertake this process the person that I was practicing on, another Bi-Aura student, or tutor, started to look green in color and feel sick, and I had to stop.

As much as I tried I could not get this process to work to my advantage using the accredited methodology, especially during the final practical examination where I got more and more flustered and was losing confidence by the moment. To be assessed we were paired up with our fellow students. We had to demonstrate to roving examiners every technique on the other, in turn. In one incident, I was acting as the 'client', before my turn to be assessed as the 'healer'. I had never carried out this particular exercise successfully and could feel myself becoming frozen with fear. So while my fellow student was working on my energy field I asked for CB to join me for the next exercise so that I could have her help; I was desperate to do well and pass my exam. I sought her help with a pure heart; I believed she would guide me in the right way. Was this cheating? I don't know. All I do know is that at the precise moment that I called out for help to CB in my mind, my fellow student who was in the role of healer said to me: "What's happened to you? Your energy field has expanded hugely, I can't get near you." And he really couldn't. A new energy field had suddenly opened up and my body was contained within it, which made it impossible for him to penetrate. This external validation of CB comforted me and gave me confidence.

When it was my turn to take on the role of the healer, I asked again for her help and I was able to carry out the technical exercise without any issues of concern to my examiners. In fact, I passed the exam with high marks.

I found the Bi-Aura training gave me a technical framework and a methodology to carry out my work as a healer. It has been one of the most helpful of the training programs I have undertaken so far.

I would like to speak a little about some of the most important lessons that I learnt both on the course and as practitioner. As I am bound by confidentiality I am not able to recount what happens when I work with clients, but I can report feedback:

I always leave Wendy's so much more lighter and more empowered than when I arrive. During the session, she works on many different levels and creates a safe space where you can be held. Wendy also gives you tools to take home with you so you can take your healing into your own hands. She has helped me through a tough period in my life by working with me and allowing me to discover my own inner strength and uncover what my truest self desires. I highly recommend her!
– Laura, Translator

I have found deep healing and release combined with a continuing sense of guidance from the work we did together,

Wendy. Thank you so very much. All the work and information was accurate and extremely effective. Your Angel is indeed 'Heaven Sent', my love! CB's timing for me was spot on, exactly as she predicted. I had an immediate resonance with Celestial Bell and truly benefited from the healings. I'm so glad I chose the package deal. I am a different woman, really returning to life and you both gave me faith to achieve this, going from strength-to-strength. Thank you once again, I'm so glad I found you.
– Liz, Healer

It is my experience that when I have been facilitating healing things really do begin to become extraordinary. Again, like Alice, when she was falling down the rabbit hole, sometimes these events are so extraordinary that the only recourse both my client and myself have is to regard them as ordinary, otherwise how would we cope? I can truly say during healing sessions both my clients and I have seen negative energy 'whoosh' away out of clients. We have seen Angels. I have seen years drop off the faces of my clients. One person came in unable to lift her hand above shoulder height and went out being able to hold it above her head. I have also learnt that engaging with the world of healing and spirituality doesn't make me immune from danger. If anything I have had to learn to be more careful because when I am open to Spirit I can be less grounded and therefore vulnerable. For example, as I will recount later, once while giving readings my handbag was stolen. I don't think that CB came into my life to enable me to abdicate responsibility for myself. I know that I must take care of myself. And that is by being contained, disciplined, present and grounded.

Here are some other things that I have learnt working as an Angel Channeler, Energy Healer and Intuitive Coach which I would like to share with you.

All healing and channeling should be a mechanism for

empowerment and not an imposition. This is what makes it a skilled and delicate craft. If there is nothing else in this book that you take away, let it be this message: both healing and channeling are aids to empowerment and growth; not mechanisms for disempowerment and dependency.

With regards to your relationship with your healer or channeler, or your own personal Angel, if you feel that you are imposed upon or being directed against your will, or if something doesn't feel right, then draw back and disengage. It's a subtle difference and really relates to power. The Healer or Channeler must have worked on their own personal issues and have the ability to disengage and draw back. Put simply it's the difference between being in a codependent relationship or in true love. The first feels heavy and the second feels light. A codependent relationship may contain elements of abuse, whereas true love contains freedom.

CB teaches me again and again to nullify or remove myself. Often a client will come and tell me their dilemma. I may start coaching or interpreting or sympathizing but if I ask CB I will get a completely different view. I need to remember the client is not coming to hear from me, they are coming to hear from CB. Whichever judgment I may want to rush to experience has taught me to draw back and really listen and take notice of what the client is saying and of what CB is saying. Healing is a sacred act. In accepting healing the client is giving a gift. This is something that I as a healer try to hold at the core of my consciousness. I am always doing my best to work at my highest possible level and draw myself back.

With regards to achieving connection to your Angel, I have learnt not to be too prescriptive. I have permission from my friend Sarah to include this case study. Sarah came to visit; she wanted to be able to reach and connect with her Angel more clearly. She asked me to explain how I did it. I tuned in to CB who showed me a picture of Sarah singing in front of an audience, completely lit up and channeling Angelic energy. Then another picture of Sarah channeling accurate information which she couldn't possibly divine without spiritual help when reading Tarot Cards. I duly relayed to Sarah that she was already channeling but just not in the same way as me. I requested that she allow and acknowledge my gift; after all I cannot sing or speak a foreign language. My talent appears to be accessing CB quickly. She saw the truth in that and agreed that the room lit up when she was leading singing and that she went into a bit of a trance when she read Tarot.

Another factor I take into consideration while undertaking healing is how appropriate it is to give clairvoyant messages. Not everyone likes to receive these; some people can see them as frightening. Before starting a session, I usually say something like, "It's not unknown for me to receive a message from Spirit. If I do would you like me to give it to you?" Then it's up to the client. I adopt the same methodology in relation to past life experiences. Several times when healing, CB has given me a glimpse of the client's past life; if it has been impacting on this one then I welcome this information because of the light that it shines upon the situation of the individual who may not be living to their potential. But again I seek permission before giving this information.

I have explained, I am now at a stage when I am able to contact my Angel instantly by calling CB in my head. I will then ask her for what I want. This is usually a message or guidance or help with giving a client healing. I think that this 'asking' is important as Angels are not allowed to intervene in our affairs, they must be asked. While I do not often ask for material things, I will ask for practical assistance if I really need it; usually this is when giving healing. Incidentally, to begin with I used to worry that I was overtaxing CB by constantly tuning in. I would apologize. However, it seems that she has a large energy field and it's not a problem to draw down on her when I need to. Now

I am so much more at ease when contacting her; there are less instances of her approaching me – although she does sometimes; but in a much more low-key way than the instances that I had when I didn't know about her.

I have also learnt to remember that giving healing or giving readings to family and friends should be undertaken with caution. Here's why. First it's almost impossible to draw back and be objective in relation to someone that you love. Anxiety and your own best wishes for the person can get in the way, and that makes it hard to receive clear messages. Also, it's important if giving treatment to family and friends to be structured, otherwise something important may be missed. Early on in my career as a healer I learnt a lesson that I have not ever forgotten, although there was no real harm done. I gave a treatment to friend of my son and left her at the end of it without fully debriefing that she may undergo a detoxing process at the end of the healing. This was because I had to attend to something. The outcome was that she wasn't fully aware that a person may need rest after healing; she was exhausted for three days and felt so wiped out that she went to have tests at the hospital. In the end, the healing was awesome and she made an amazing recovery, but I would not have treated a client in this way. It was unnecessary that she experienced anxiety.

Another issue when treating family and friends is their capacity to trust you enough to receive the message that you are giving, particularly if they perceive it's in your interest. The last thing that you want is for a friend or family member to perceive you as controlling. Don't forget it is difficult enough, especially for your children or partner, that your psychic ability causes weird things to happen around you and they can't get away with much either, because you just know.

I also discovered that Bi-Aura Healing is not restricted to people but may be used more widely; this story doesn't concern a person at all. It concerns a car and a safe. It was my 51st birthday and friends had made me a birthday tea party, mainly I think because I had been unbearably miserable and they wanted to cheer me up. I arrived at the party at the same time as one friend and noticed that she was shuffling over from the driver's side of the car to climb out the passenger's door. She told me that the driver's side door lock was completely stuck, which of course meant that the door wouldn't open.

Strangely, as she told me this, my hand started to grow hot, as it often does when healing is needed. So I walked over to the side of the car and I gave the door lock standard Bi-Aura Healing as if it were a person. Immediately, the lock clicked up and then the driver's door could be opened. Very cool. This cheered me up and made my birthday even better. Healing mechanical things is so rewarding because it offers demonstrable evidence rather than relying on humans to recount back their feelings. So I came back from my tea party happier than when I went but then my friends were also very lovely. Of course, I told my sons of my triumph. Josh then told me that in the bar where he worked the lock of the safe had been jammed closed for six months. Although it contained money, the money within was equal to the expense of having a locksmith break open the safe so it remained closed.

Once I heard this story I then became desperate to have a go at opening that safe. Every time I went past the building my hand became hot and tingled. Josh, however, was adamant that I shouldn't try. It was his place of work. If I failed he would be embarrassed. Eventually one day I called in for coffee and Josh took pity on me. He asked his manager if I could try to open the safe. So I went behind the bar to the office. I had had specific instructions; CB said what I needed to open the safe was in the desk. First, I asked for olive oil. Oddly, for a restaurant they didn't have any. I remembered the desk and looked in a drawer and found some hand cream. I rubbed the hand cream onto the safe's key, gave the lock Bi-Aura Healing and it opened straightaway! The money was retrieved and I was given 10% as a commission. This was pleasing. Practical friends laugh at this story and dispute that there was Angelic influence. They ask me if I haven't heard of WD-40. Or say that of course it opened; it was just a sticky lock. Put hand cream on it and it will open. However, I have faith. I know that it was CB; I knew in advance that something else was needed besides the Bi-Aura. Besides which a locksmith had also tried to open the safe and failed, presumably using WD-40 rather than 'Angel juice'.

Just to show that I was on the right track when I started to write about this incident in this book today, the text turned into the color purple like this as I was typing. There was absolutely no reason for it to do so. It has never happened before or since; my Apple Mac is working fine. I certainly didn't change the font. The only rationale for it that I can come up with is that purple is the color of spirituality and I was being shown by CB that yes it was her helping me to open the safe and that I should have more faith.

We can learn from the fact that as our spirit descends to be on the Earth our connection to Spirit is naturally restricted. As we are spiritual beings having a human experience we are supposed to be having a life! It is not practical to be constantly connected. In metaphysical parlance, it's called being open. The danger of being continually open is being ungrounded. I am speaking from harsh experience here. I have already mentioned the stolen handbag. But I once lost valuable jewelry in a park. I took off my necklace and a ring to give healing on an impulse. I put them on a bench and then after giving the healing I forgot to close my connection. I was so blissed out and dreamy that I left the jewelry on the park bench. Another time I came out of a training session and forgot to close my Crown Chakra[1] because I had had half a bottle of wine the night before, and alcohol and healing do not mix. The outcome was that I was so spaced out coming home I got on the wrong train by mistake and ended up in Southampton. It took me eight hours to get back to Totnes!

As you can see, 'grounding and closing' are very important in the process of closing the Crown Chakra after healing sessions: I have put an example of an exercise to be able to do this in a chapter of its own: It follows next!

Chapter Three

When training to be a healer I was taught to close my Crown Chakra after healing or channeling. One way to do this is to imagine that you are a car and that you have opened the sunroof to connect to Spirit: when you have finished the session close the sunroof. Or if you prefer, think of the image of a thousand-leaved lotus flower on the top of your head. Imagine it opening to receive Spirit and then when you have finished your meditation shut the leaves into a tight bud to close the connection to Spirit and be grounded.

I cannot emphasize enough the importance of this simple exercise. It may not sound like much, but not closing is the equivalent of walking out of your house and leaving the front door open! And just as risky. It is one thing if you are consciously meditating or raising your vibration to connect with Angels, quite another to wander around open and by so doing losing control and allowing anything into your being. It is easy to forget that spiritual work has its dangers. The opening of the esoteric world has taken the work away from where it was originally contained within the disciplined world of priests and priestesses.

I am all for making Spirit accessible, for encouraging a spiritual journey. This is the journey of our age, to integrate the spiritual with material. I learnt the hard way to be disciplined within this. I would urge you to put a practice in place that ensures that you close down and ground yourself after you work.

If you find after your spiritual work that you are still feeling dreamy, even after closing energetically, then a quick way to ground is to drink water, or eat something sweet; stamp your feet and move around. Clap your hands or brush the top of your head while saying, "Come back. Come back." Or imagine that roots are growing out of your feet down into the earth. Draw up some of the red energy of the Earth back up the roots and see it staying in your body up to your waist.

Chapter Four

Celestial Bell has in many channeled readings over the last five years been speaking about "The Great Shift", which I understand as a time when our life on Earth will change for the better. I have also channeled that this will include the integration of material and spiritual, and of the masculine and feminine. I began to realize that CB was speaking about the move to a 'New World', one that operates at a higher level, a world that is post-2012; that all along what was meant by 2012, ushering in the 'end of the world', was an end of a fragmented way of being.

I understand that we as a human race are all hungry and all homeless if we have just one person hungry or a single person without a roof over their head. It is in all of our interests to raise the world to a level of happiness and joy, but above all safety and security and nourishment beyond hunger. But how do we do it? Easily said, less easily done? Or perhaps it is easily done? Step by step? Action by action? Loving kindness by loving kindness? This is the concept Gandhi spoke of: "Be the change that you wish to see in the world."[2]

As one of my close friends says to me often, "It's an inside job"; the best place to start with improvement of the world is with our own self. That is in part why I have undertaken my own personal journey of change. Because I want to see change in the world, I have decided first to change myself. I want to feel, and I also want others to feel and notice the change in me as a good example. Perhaps each person embarking on a spiritual pathway to change is crisscrossing the world and heralding in collective change by means of their individual efforts and progress.

As we undertake spiritual work surely this change must be reflected in the world as a whole? Thus as the individual shifts then so does the world? Of course the complete revolution in technology is an enormous aid to this; access to ICT and telecommunication has the potential to be an equalizer. I understand it as a concrete manifestation of a collective consciousness; even if at the time of writing access is unequal.

But how does this change impact upon us? What happens when we integrate the material and the spiritual? What does it all mean? I was helped to understand what CB meant by integration of the spiritual and material by some of the experiences of my clients in Watkins Books in Central London.

Three things struck me. First was that once 'enlightened', people were often torn between being in a 'spiritual' career or 'conventional' career (and I have experienced difficulty myself). Secondly, the care that we need to take when we are undertaking spiritual practices while operating in a material world. And thirdly, that spiritual integration with the material involves us all in paying attention to integrated process.

One question in particular brought many people to the velvet-covered table in Watkins Books. That of "What next?" "I want to know what to do." "I have studied and qualified as a yoga teacher, reiki healer… now should I give up my day job and open a center somewhere… in France?" I ask, "What do you do?" They respond, "I am an artist." "I work in the Civil Service." "I sell wine." "I teach." "Now, I am discontented, my eyes are open and I have (spiritual) work to do. That will mean no money! But I feel it is my calling but I will have no money, what should I do?"

Then I ask: "Do you like your work?" "Yes, I love it," they say. I ask CB to give insight into whether or not a change of direction will support this person's journey. If the person is happy in their work nine times out of ten the advice is to remain in it in order to "assist The Shift and aid the integration." Because eyes have been opened and spirituality accessed there is no reason to abandon the mainstream. On the contrary, we need as many spiritual teachers, artists, wine sellers, bankers etc. as we can get to bring light to the darkness.

The mainstream is astonishing in its ability to absorb and

make conventional the unconventional. Just look at how 'glamping' it up at the Glastonbury Festival every year has entered the national vocabulary; how 'mindfulness' techniques in the workplace become mainstream; the quest for a spiritual oasis in the material world. It is fascinating at how a new language is developing to allow acceptability of the spiritual, magical world. Glamping? Mindfulness? Then there is the world of JK Rowling's *Harry Potter* and what insights we gather from the spiritual references and magical illusions in this work of fiction that has snowballed into an international phenomenon which has more meaning for many than mere entertainment. Suddenly concepts and what they stand for – such as 'witch night bus', 'Diagon Alley' and 'Muggles' – become integrated into the mass consciousness, along with the core concept of JK Rowling's work, which celebrates the power of a mother's love empowering an orphan to overcome an evil aggressor.

It seems to me that if you are assisting with 'The Great Shift' by getting more involved in spiritual pursuits then you may be on a mission to take the light into a place that was previously dark. While that may or may not mean a change or advancement in a professional career, it does mean that there is a need to be spiritually and emotionally strong; to keep your wits about you; lead by example; and have faith. There may be times when others find your loving energy threatening and may try to oust you. It also might involve a strategic skill, for although the spiritual is currently being absorbed it does not mean that it has yet had the paradigm shift that we need for it to become mainstream and accessible to more people.

On the other hand, sometimes it is appropriate to make the shift to earning a living in the metaphysical world. For many years, I denied my spirituality and denied the fact that I could do more to support the Earth by assisting others through healing, channeling, intuitive coaching and energy work. There was a time when I liked having a paid, secure job in a government office. And then I enjoyed running my own business. But those days are over now. My calling is in a new direction. I am and I want to be a Mystic. This is what I was created to do and so I am!

When clients come to the table in Watkins Books in confusion, they may feel that they have a calling. They report to me while they have well-paid jobs they are unhappy; they "know" there is more to life than a high-paid job or a job that they do not really like but know they must do due to social or familial pressure or demands. When working with these clients CB will often advise that they cross the bridge from one sector to another slowly and imperceptibly dropping one day a week in their mainstream work and building up work in the area of their interest. Sometimes, however, she advises a complete change. It all depends upon the person and their circumstances. CB is the most practical Angel!

If the change will involve a reduction in money, if for example working in a high-powered highly-paid sector such as banking or advertising and wanting perhaps to move to the third sector, charity or voluntary work, CB will often advise for the person to make a gentle, slow shift; a change for the better; a change that aligns them closer to their true calling, their true passion and need. But I never underestimate the trickiness of making change and the courage it takes especially if large amounts of resource have been devoted to building up a career in a stable and/or prestigious line of work. It takes a brave person to step out of being a doctor and retrain as an artist, for example.

Here is CB's insight:

"Follow the heart, work to fulfill your deepest dreams. Each day that you have is an opportunity for expressing the Divine. Expression of the Divine is based upon happiness. Always remember that each person is both a miracle and capable of making a miracle. Dance in the joy of the day."

Chapter Five

Part of my self-acceptance as a psychic *or mystic* also came from understanding what my lifework is. This is the work that my soul contracted to deliver during this lifetime before I was born. If you haven't found your lifework yet I suggest that you stop everything now! And go and find it immediately! Once you have it it's incredibly empowering. The insight that I offer is that when presented with your lifework you will, if it's true, recognize it at a deep level.

Often clients come ask me to ask my Angel to tell them what their lifework should be. Although CB will sometimes tell me, I much prefer to facilitate clients to look within themselves for the answer. It's what I did to find my lifework.

In the first section of this book, I told you the story of the shadow of the oil lamp flame I discovered in the tomb in Jerusalem (page 21) and the effect it had on me. I left Israel soon after this experience to embark on a spiritual quest that included spiritual training and the acceptance of my own personal Angel. Years later, I undertook a guided meditation and was shown by a facilitator how to focus my lifework. I was told that my task is to bring joy to others through my spiritual work. This I do today with much happiness as it brings much joy into my life to work this way.

It has taken me longer than my personal Angel hoped to come to many realizations about my abilities and the job I must undertake as a psychic and mystic. I admit I resisted the work. I was frightened by the psychic experiences I had as a small child; I didn't understand what was going on, but today I do. And I am pleased I possess the spiritual and emotional abilities that God so kindly granted me. The gift of my personal Angel Celestial Bell has augmented my journey to self-acceptable and self-actualization; without her I could not give the best of me.

Without continual training in my field I could not give the best of me to my clients and readers.

Today, I feel happy when I tell anyone who asks my profession that I am an Angel Channeler, Energy Healer and Intuitive Coach. That I also write and teach in my chosen field. The extraordinary aspect of finding my lifework is that I live it day-to-day just like an ordinary day; it is part of everything I do and feel. I simply love what I do, so it is not work anymore; I truly do spend my days living my lifework.

When I see a client who apologizes for taking my time, or apologizes for the burden of removing toxic energy or is concerned about aspects of their life that are negative as they seek me to help them live in the positive, I smile and thank my client and thank God for the work I do. I see my lifework as an absolute privilege; I regard my work as sacred. Since I trained and equipped myself to manage and actualize my psychic abilities and skills I feel contained with boundless energy to undertake my work. While I enjoy all the work I do, the work I particularly enjoy and see the greatest benefit for my clients from is Realignment Therapy; this enables my client to access the Divine and feel in-balance. The purpose of all my work is to offer Angelic healing, facilitation and guidance in order to enable each client to realize their potential and be realigned with Source Energy. Realignment Therapy is the foundation from which further more specific healing can take flight.

When I meet a client, I am not sure what is going to happen until we start working together; the soul is different every moment, and the needs of the soul shift accordingly. Therefore it is hard to know what will happen on any one occasion. I work on an intuitive level; there is no prescription. I offer, if you like, Bespoke Healing; tailor-made to suit the client's needs at any particular time. This is because every person is unique; and every soul has its need. Sometimes all that is needed is instruction in how to manage energy, or assistance with clearing.

The day my personal Angel presented me with an image of a Seer in the National Gallery was the day I began to finally accept my lifework. I realized I was a psychic and I had a responsibility to educate and train myself accordingly. That day in 2012, I accepted my true calling. This acceptance is now reflected back to me in all the work I do with my clients.

Chapter Six

In 1998, in my capacity as a local government officer specializing in Social Housing I visited the Houses of Parliament to speak with MPs about how to promote Local Exchange Trading Schemes and Credit Unions.[3] On this day, along with two other colleagues we had an appointment at 2pm to proceed with our approved activist agenda.

On arrival at the House of Commons, I recall standing in the vast Westminster Hall, the center of power in all of England. Looking up high in the rafters and seeing the faces of many carved Angels looking down, I found out later that there are twenty-six Angels in total. They were carved in 1399 when the roof of Westminster Hall was rebuilt.

Without consciously realizing it, I see Angels everywhere! Angels form a backdrop to our everyday lives; and we rarely even notice them! While many of us use the word 'angel' nonchalantly or as a term of endearment, more and more people are realizing Angels are serious business. They exist, they have value and we exist in their midst; but how much more effective and special our lives become when we live with Angels and form a working and effective relationship with them!

You might have heard someone say: "You are an Angel." It is an accepted expression these days, an expression of gratitude to someone who has extended kindness to you. In these times of great planetary change, and also for many people like myself who work actively with the Higher Realms, Angels are part of our everyday lives; they bring us great comfort and help us help others and ourselves.

Since I formed a positive and productive union with my personal Angel, I have felt more beloved, supported and blessed. As I grow older and wiser – I hope – I realize the value of an Angel in my life to guide myself and those around me that are open to the miracle and nature of this type of intervention and support. Because you really have to be open to this type of intervention and support, it is not for everyone; I realize that. But the way I look at it is each of us is on a journey from the moment we arrive into this world; we are passing through the material world to return to the spiritual world. Therefore how much more pleasant the journey is for me now with an Angel to accompany me; and to think Celestial Bell was there from the very beginning, and I feel for sure she will be there as I pass through to the next world, where I have this feeling I am going to be in good company.

There is more evidence for Angels in the world I live in than I expected. There was a time about four years ago, when I was quite active in my local Jewish community in Totnes, Devon, where I lived and plan on returning to this springtime.

In 2011, my local community was bequeathed the gift of a 24-volume set of *The Kabbalah*, better known as *The Zohar*[4] – the holy, mystical writings of the Jewish faith. When the volume set arrived it initially was stored in the study in our home. *The Zohar* are sacred books; even the act of having the books present in our house raised the spiritual vibration. The word *Zohar* in Hebrew translates into: splendor or radiance.

During the time period we were custodians of these holy books I was being urged by CB to hurry up and read Volume One of *The Zohar*; our edition was in Hebrew with an English translation. Eventually, after much prompting I sat down one day to begin the work of reading very carefully and thoroughly material that astonished me which contained continual references to both Astrology and to Angels.

To be honest, this discovery was a relief; until this point in my life I had incorrectly assumed that Astrology and Angels were terms and references outside of the realm of Judaism; that Angels particularly were not integrated into the Jewish belief system and were at odds with the spiritual realms outside of this faith. Surprised and relieved, I read on to learn more about the role and purpose of the Angels in our midst. It would be remiss of me not to put a strict warning in here. *The Zohar* is not a book for all mankind to read; it has holy powers and must be read only at a certain age, and – I understand now – should be read preferably in a group situation under careful guidance from a learned mentor or teacher, for there to be clear understanding of the meaning behind the text so that misunderstanding and misinterpretation does not occur. 'Handle with Care' is the best term I can think of to anyone considering investing time studying this collection of holy, mystical teachings.

So in plain terms, what is an Angel – anyway? Strangely enough, even though I have been conscious of my own personal Angel since I was a small child I did not undertake formal study of Angels until I came across *The Zohar*. The definition of an Angel is 'Being of Light'. In Volume One of *The Zohar* there are references to Angels; the writings expound upon their place in the universe. It appears that the function of an Angel is to be a messenger between God – or the Divine Essence – and humans because 'The Light of God' is too unbelievably pure for us humans to manage; writings that delve deep into sections of the Old Testament tell us that we could not possibly look upon the 'Face of God' without becoming blind; the 'Light of God' is too bright for us to fathom. The best way to imagine what I am talking about is to visualize when a person is in the wilderness, a desert for example, and they are wandering lost beneath the hot sun: they are parched for water and delirious. The sun is at midday and scorching. One tries to raise their eyes to look into the sun and one has to cover their eyes; the sun is much too bright even to look at. I guess that is what it must be like but probably a million times more powerful!

The Zohar explains that as God is unable to communicate with us directly He appoints Angels as intermediaries. This is because the light of the Divine or the light of God is too bright for us humans to be able to look at. In very simple terms, as I find this information so overwhelmingly awesome to rationalize, Angels absorb and dilute 'The Light of God' as an act of kindness so that Angels can come into our midst to be of help and comfort to us. You may think I am talking of Angels rather casually here, and that they are easy to explain. This could not be further from the truth. I, and most of the people in this universe, am not in a position to understand or even comprehend for a moment the absolute ways of God. But, God is in our midst, and one way God manifests is through ambassadors: Angels. Religious and spiritual writings in *all religions* assert this fact.

From personal experience, I know my personal Angel exists. From studying holy and spiritual writings, I also know Angels exist as I gather more knowledge and understanding – and respect – for the ways of God, and the ways of Angels. The more I work with my clients, the more I also gain respect and understanding for the ways of mankind. Truly we human beings are blessed; even more so when we have a personal Angel watching over us and guiding us.

I continue to study holy and spiritual writings yet I am still unclear where my personal Angel fits into the hierarchy within the realm of the Archangels as described in *The Zohar* and currently being discussed and acknowledged within the forum of Metaphysics by contemporary Angel writers such as Lorna Byrne or Doreen Virtue.[5] When I ask my personal Angel Celestial Bell where she fits in, I receive a feeling of stretching; CB tells me that she simply "just is". It feels as if there is puzzlement in relation to our conception of hierarchies.

I want to make it very clear here that when my personal Angel talks to me I may only get impressions to pass onto the client. I may not get specific information or directions. Sometimes I do not possess the language to put everything that I sense and I am shown into words, as the way the material is presented to me is far outside of my reality to comprehend; sometimes I do not have a framework that allows the vision as a possibility.

Chapter Seven

An Angel Channeler communicates knowledge through the world of Angels. From my research and from personal experience, it appears that each individual Angel has a 'consciousness', an energy that it is possible to draw down upon. Not only that, but also this 'consciousness' is entirely capable of independently providing assistance if and when required. This assistance may be given simultaneously to many individuals at the same time without effort, which is incredibly miraculous. The reality or perception is that each Archangel has a particular remit.

Each of my sons attended the South Devon Steiner School. Here pupils are taught according to the principles of Anthroposophy. This is a philosophy founded by Rudolf Steiner. Steiner postulated the existence of an objective, intellectually comprehensible spiritual world accessible to direct experience through inner development. Anthroposophical ideas have been applied practically in many areas including Steiner/Waldorf education, special education (most prominently through the Camphill Movement), biodynamic agriculture, medicine, ethical banking, organizational development, and the arts.

As an adult I have also been educated at this school, learning alongside my children; parents are very involved in the day-to-day running of the school. There is an abundance of accumulated wisdom within both the teaching body and the parent body of the school. Raphaela Cooper,[6] an artist, who was once a school parent, is also an Angel Channeler. Raphaela, with her innate understanding of Angels, wrote the following explanation of Archangels. It is reproduced in full with her permission:

Many people have become familiar with the idea that each individual being is accompanied in life with an individual Guardian Angel. Other Angels work in families, small communities and institutions. Individual Archangels have a larger remit and role. They have extensive responsibilities, which include guiding the destiny of whole nations. According to ancient esoteric traditions there are also seven leading Archangels that carry very special tasks, which are related to specific rhythms of time in history. These traditions link these seven beings to particular planets; the nature of the planet involved bestows particular powers that leave their imprint in different periods of history.

There are seven Archangels that rotate in the same order, like days of the week, each covering an earthly span of time of approximately 354 years. If we go back two millennia we see the following influences: Orphiel, the Saturn Archangel, 246 BC–AD 108; Anael, the Venus Archangel, 108 AD–463 AD; Zachariel, the Jupiter Archangel, 463 AD–817 AD; Raphael, the Mercury Archangel, 817 AD until 1171 AD; Samael, the Mars Archangel, 1523–1879. Currently we are living within the span of the Sun Archangel Mikel, 1879 until the current time. Orphiel returns in a new cycle about the year 2231.

I encountered the sacred realm of Archangels myself in quite an ordinary manner.

One morning when we met for coffee Raphaela was holding a piece of paper. She had received an e-mail from John Levine who is a composer of alpha music.[7] Levine had produced a series of Archangel CDs and was looking for a volunteer to help promote them at the November 2011 Mind Body Spirit Festival in the Royal Horticultural Halls. Raphaela was insistent that I should do it. She said that the e-mail had jumped out at her "with my name on it". I felt an enormous pull to go; I would also earn a set of Angel CDs. I contacted John Levine and subsequently went to London to promote the Archangel Series.

At the show I found that the environment for selling the CDs wasn't that easy.

I love meeting people and I enjoy selling but there I was on a busy stall with a tiny space. Not only that, opposite me someone was promoting and demonstrating 'Gong Therapy' – not exactly quietly – and to my left there was a stall selling drums which was also holding 'on the floor' drumming workshops; there were a few challenging aspects to being on the stand.

But I didn't need to worry; help was at hand and I immediately began to hear and be aware of Archangel Jophiel. I experienced Jophiel as a light and joyous energy – reminding me of a bubbling brook, rising up and in bursts of joy. I couldn't stop giggling the whole time that I was on the stand. The role of Archangel Jophiel is to represent the beauty of God. Archangel Jophiel supports the third Chakra (Solar Plexus), which is yellow in color and relates to Personal Power. The affirmation of the Solar Plexus is – 'The Right to Act'. Jophiel encouraged me to sell the CDs by dowsing.

This is how I did it. I used a healing technique designed for humans on the CDs! The Bi-Aura Healing course taught me that all living things including ourselves have an energy field, which is Chi, Energy Force. It may also be referred to as an 'etheric field'.

You can discover your Chi by briskly rubbing your hands together, holding them apart at a distance of about two meters and then, with palms facing each other, gently bringing your hands together. Before your palms meet you should feel a warmth or bounce – this is the energy that surrounds you, to about an arm's length; it is delightful, beautiful, and feeling it should cause you to feel warm inside and smile.

If the concept of Chi, Energy Force is new to you and you would like to explore further you might like to sit at a table with some living things in front of you: fruit or a plant, or perhaps a crystal. Find your own Chi, Energy Force as explained. Now hold your hand palm facing down above the fruit or plant or crystal, and gently push down towards it. You should feel the energy field of the fruit or plant or crystal gently resisting you; and not only that, you will also experience the subtle differences in energy of each living thing. It is also possible to feel the energy of original paintings or sculpture.

I held my hand above each of the Archangel CDs. I found that there was an energetic charge. John Levine had channeled the music for each of the 12 Archangels in succession in a cathedral in Krakow in Poland. Along with the widely known Michael, Gabriel and Raphael, common to the three Abrahamic faiths, Levine was guided to channel Ariel, Chamuel, Haniel, Jophiel, Metatron, Uriel, Raguel, Sandalphon and Zadkiel.

I have seen photos of John Levine composing this music, and orbs are in evidence. I am grateful for his innate generosity and desire to improve all of our quality of life through his healing music that works on a Vibrational level.

At the Mind Body Spirit show, as we were challenged and unable to hear the music because there was so much noise around us, I took Jophiel's advice and sold the CDs by dowsing, through simply asking people to hold their hand above the stand and see which Archangel had the greatest draw or charge. Everyone I assisted was able to do this; they all knew by the degree of charge or instinct which was the right Angel CD for them. Some people felt an equal charge from all the CDs and they bought the whole set. The purpose of the music on the CDs is to raise the vibration in the room and be able to invoke the individual Archangel. Please remember that these are powerful CDs – they put the listener into a semi-trance – so are to be used with care and definitely not when driving.

Chapter Eight

One summer day in 2015, Raphaela and I sat in her garden to speak about Angels and their impact on our day-to-day life. The section that follows is a compilation of our discussion. I have included it to give you a general orientation into the profile of an Archangel as well as assist you in calling upon an Archangel of your choice. I encourage you to do further research if any of the following introductory information piques your interest.

Archangel Ariel: Archangel Ariel is closely associated with the realm of nature spirits; you may find her to be slightly ethereal and hard to define but you will know that she is there. Her energy is light and her colors are all the colors of the rainbow.

Related Chakra: Sacral concerning sexuality and creativity.

This is my personal experience of this realm: In January 2015, I gave an Angel reading session to an artist/author who works with nature spirits. She was in the process of writing a book about nature spirits. During the reading I saw her heart covered with tiny nature spirits. It was the first time that I have ever been given a glimpse of this realm. I believe that I was being given this privilege to help her as while she is seen as an expert in the field, she was still finding it difficult to find the right words to describe this realm; my task at the time was to give her faith and encouragement. I am not even going to attempt to channel Ariel and give a written message. I know that I will not be able to translate any messages through her. The impression that I get when I try and reach this energy is one of heightened awareness, of lights moving around that cannot be pinned down. There is a sense of holding my breath and listening intently. I know that the Archangel Ariel wishes to remind us of our duty to honor the Earth and be respectful to the elementals that we may not be able to see but nonetheless are there and entitled to holy respect.

Archangel Chamuel or Samuel: Archangel Chamuel is linked to the planet Mars. He is especially helpful if you need energy, or the will to get something started or completed; helps with innovative projects. Chamuel will help soldiers in righteous battles. He helps bring things into being when that final effort is needed, for the last push. Chamuel will assist in any personal battle. His color is red.

Related Chakra: the Root. The Root Chakra concerns material well-being, in terms of having our basic needs met: food, shelter, money, survival.

The Archangel Chamuel also assists us in reaching and manifesting the Divine through unconditional love. When I feel that I may be lured into chasing after material things to give me happiness I ask Archangel Chamuel to help me by giving me balance. I also remind myself of the late American author Maya Angelou's words: "I've learned that people will forget what you said, people will forget what you did, but people will never forget how you made them feel."[8] Unconditional love has the potential to raise us to Heaven.

Archangel Gabriel: Archangel Gabriel is beloved of mothers and children. He works to enhance the brain and the third eye, helping to introduce the new clairvoyance that comes as part of the 'Great Shift'. His task is to help with transformation and assist us to create Heaven on Earth as well as helping to protect pregnant women and aid parents to understand their children and the gifts that their children bring. Related Chakra is the Brow. Colors: purple and silver. The Brow Chakra concerns our ability to see and understand the truth; this is rational truth as well as the third eye. Hence Archangel Gabriel also assists us in integration. You many ask him to help and comfort your inner child; especially a wounded inner child.

Here is my channeled message from the Archangel Gabriel: "Use your power well and with care. Understand your magnificence. You are all capable of achieving great things. Allow your light to shine out upon the Earth. Assist in its healing. Every drop of water contains an ocean, as do you."

Related Chakra: Sacral. Color: orange.

Archangel Haniel: Archangel Haniel is the Archangel of miracles; he works to relieve suffering and bring about miraculous solutions; he is helpful in times of dire need.

Related Chakra: Heart. Color: dazzling white.

Archangel Metatron: The Archangel Metatron supports our work that concerns the repair of the world; through the act of giving and the ability to receive, balance is maintained and we become whole and strong. Archangel Metatron is important to this book, which concerns the integration of the material with spiritual to obtain our balance and rightful place and duty on Earth. When I connect to the Archangel Metatron I do not receive words, I am granted a vision of a spine. The emphasis is upon his presence in the foundation of our infrastructure; how he helps us stand upright in truth and integrity, by realizing our capacity to make manifest the Divine through the root of our strength and intelligence, for the spine upholds the body and our intelligence.

Related Chakra: Root. Color: red.

Archangel Mikel or Michael: Archangel Mikel is the Sun Archangel and the current leader of Archangels which is why he is sometimes referred to as 'the Angel of our Time'. He helps with authenticity, enabling us to speak our truth. He also brings the rational into the heart and is helping us to expand the heart chakra to a higher realm; changing it from green to peach blossom pink. This transformation of the heart enables it to become an organ of intelligence, to assist humanity with enhanced intuition and greater compassion, helping to usher in the time of 'The Great Shift' post-2012. Call upon Archangel Mikel if you have a need for protection, strength, courage or intelligence. Also if you would like self-knowledge, to know who you really are. Mikel has troops of many angels working with him, helping to combat spirits of darkness.

Related Chakra: Heart. Colors: blue and silver.

My Note: The Archangel Mikel assists especially in having faith and achieving change, of being authentic. In our time, we need help to integrate the material and the spiritual into our lives in order to protect and assist our Earth and achieve our potential for happiness. The Archangel Mikel is the Angel in charge of this mission. Because this is a journey that involves us in resistance and struggle Archangel Mikel will, if we ask, help us. When we elect to seek out Angel Channelers and we accept the readings, we are inviting help into our lives; we are choosing to be brave and true to our times; we are asking for the help we need to make the transition we need to make to be a success both materially and spiritually. Earlier, I described how I was in despair and found help from Mikel in a dream with my friend Kim (page 37). Mikel especially gave me the strength to cope with transitioning from a materially-based existence where I was more focused on myself as an individual to being able to draw myself back, and see things from a collective viewpoint that has the needs of the whole Earth in mind. My friend Raphaela, the artist I mentioned who is a school parent from Devon, had a similar dream-related experience she wanted me to share with you:

We used to live on Wearyall Hill in Glastonbury, Somerset, England, which is a hill in the shape of a giant whale; a magical hill according to the locals. Local legend says that after the death of Jesus, Joseph of Arimathea came to the hill and planted his staff, which transformed into a holy thorn bush. Our house was close to 'this' thorn bush. Close by also lived two clairvoyants. One of these clairvoyants occupied a rose-covered cottage. One day she came up to our house and knocked on the door, and said: "Raphaela, I have something to tell you. While I was standing in my garden I had a vision of a giant troop of men on horseback coming up the hill, and the leader was shining and radiant like a giant Angel. The men stopped outside your door and one stooped down to check his horse hoof. I asked him: 'Who is your Leader?' And the rider replied: 'That is the Archangel Michael.'"

Raphaela told me that from that day she has closely felt the presence of the Archangel Michael; that she was guided by him to open the Rainbows End Cafe in Glastonbury selling whole food meals and serving as a community meeting point. Although at the conception of the project Raphaela didn't have the money to put it in place, she was lent it by her father. The business went from strength to strength, progressing with ease, and although Raphaela and her husband Christopher sold it on in order to come to Totnes in Devon to help start up The Rudolf Steiner School in Dartington, the cafe is still in existence.

Raphaela is convinced that providing and consuming good food is Angelic work because 'we are what we eat' and we need to consume good pure unsullied food to keep our vibration high and be able to connect with the Angelic realm as well as be equipped to fulfil our potential on Earth.

When I connect into the Archangel Mikel I have a sense of grandeur and stretching; of unlimited potential. Although the energy is majestic it is also nourishing. There is an encouragement to march out; be able to implement change; speak the truth even when afraid. The Archangel Mikel urges us not to be deterred, highlighting justice but also change that is sudden and fiery, uncompromising. Some situations may be difficult to navigate but assistance is available. This is a large energy that enables you to be lit from within and for inner strength.

This is the message that I channeled from the Archangel Mikel: "Children of the Earth rise and stand tall. Do not be bowed. Shine justice on all areas of darkness, work to raise vibration from within and from without. Be good to self and good to the Earth."

Archangel Raguel: This is the Archangel that helps to resolve conflicts and will assist us in fair and just decision making; enabling us to pull back and make the wisest choice. Sometimes it is hard to cope with conflict on a day-to-day basis; and we wish to run from the 'marketplace' and retreat into the spiritual. But if we are to assist the Earth in transcending to a higher vibrational plane then we need to be able to deal with conflict; to be able to hold our ground and be strong. Call upon Archangel Raguel when you have the need for moral courage that may not make you popular but is necessary in the greater scheme of things.

Related Chakras: Heart and Crown. Colors: green and silver.

My Note: When I tuned in to Archangel Raguel I had the vision of a white and perfectly-built and shining wall. Although known as the Angel of diplomacy and negotiation, most able to assist in resolving disputes, I also felt that the Archangel Raguel helps when good strong boundaries need to be put in place whether at work or in our personal lives. An energy orbits around the Archangel Raguel that speaks to me of justice, cleanliness and safety. I ask for Archangel Raguel's help when I feel the need to dispel psychic invasion as well as help in legal matters.

Archangel Raphael: The Great Healer. Raphael is the Archangel of the planet Mercury, and provides inspiration for doctors and all healers. He is concerned with balance and bringing us back

The Gift of an Angel

into balance; with the in-breath and the out-breath, he rules the heart and the lungs. The link to the winged feet of Mercury reflects the assistance that this important Archangel gives to travelers. He will assist you if you need a companion when traveling to feel safer. He will also help if you wish to raise the energy around a situation and if you either need healing or help in giving healing.

Related Chakra: Heart. Color: many shades of vibrant green.

My Note: As a healer I feel a special affinity for Raphael and have had several profound experiences involving this Archangel which I speak about in Part One, Chapter 8, and in Part Three, Chapter 7.

Archangel Sandalphon: Sandalphon is often depicted with a trumpet, used to call humans to service. He is particularly concerned with assisting light workers and volunteers who want to help humanity, wishing to inspire us with the power of love and remind us of the need to connect with the energy of the Earth in order to bring the divine into manifestation.

Connected Chakra: Root. Color: red.

My Note: The Archangel Sandalphon informs me that he offers us the service of being a plank or platform upon which to stand while bringing our gifts to the world. The power of prayer is a reminder of our ability to make manifest our hopes and needs, and of how much the Earth wishes to give to us, for the simple reason that the happier we are the more we then in turn give to the Earth.

Archangel Uriel is another Sun Archangel and rules midsummer. Uriel has the power to see where we may be doing wrong, making us aware of this so that we may put things right and act with integrity. Archangel Uriel can appear stern and is magnificent.

Related Chakras: impacts upon all Chakras. Color: gold.

Archangel Zadkiel is linked to Jupiter the great thinker and rules the realm of philosophy. This Archangel influences the great thinkers of our planet. Call upon Zadkiel for insight, wisdom and if you wish to see the broader picture. He helps us to be more upright, to work at a deeper level, and will help us if we are blocked creatively or downhearted.

Related Chakra: Brow. Color: purple.

My Note: Tuning into the Archangel Zadkiel does not allow me to give a channeled reading. Instead, I had the sense of power, focus and steadiness; of being able to step through the material plane to the spiritual realm and heighten my vibration. I felt my heart Chakra expand, and tension dissolve into awareness and compassion rather than conflict. As I was able to gain release from self-created dramas I was able to understand the perceptions of others and have greater empathy and love.

When the first draft of this book was completed, I circulated it to selected readers. Because today there is so much material available on Archangels both on the Internet and published I wasn't sure whether or not to include this section. The feedback, however, was both confirming and positive. Everyone without exception reported that they found this section useful, and not only that, many people used the knowledge given to make a difference in their everyday lives and encounter magical events.

One friend told me that she was reading the draft on a beach, tuned in to the Archangels, and then went into the sea to find that a circle of white feathers surrounded her.

My son Josh told me that he felt "warm inside and held". My friend Kim felt that her psychic ability improved; she actually turned up at my house to give me a reading, telling me to have faith in my efforts, that this book would have a wide audience and not to worry about the lack of consultancy work while I was working on it. This was helpful. I was exhausted after the first draft, full of tears and doubt and overwhelmed. It was sensible for Angels to send Kim with these messages; she is pragmatic and down to earth. I listen to her because she is exceptionally organized.

I think it is important here to tell you how to talk to Archangels. It is not difficult or complicated. You simply spend a little time acquainting yourself with their name and qualities; then you find a quiet place and envision the Angel bearing in mind what you have learned about the Angel. You can then open a dialogue in your words with the Angel, speaking very plainly, telling the Angel your feelings and needs. Sometimes you will want to reach out to an Angel at the most unquiet time, in a time of chaos or in a crowded room. Do not resist; do not hold back. Know that you can call on an Angel at any time of day or night; they are 'on duty' 24/7! They exist to serve you.

So enjoy and keep me posted on any news and special stories you would like to share with me; you will find my contact details on page 169 of this book.

Chapter Nine

I had another Angel experience involving the CDs when I joined John Levine to give a talk about them at the NutriCentre, a whole food store in London. I thought that I was only going to be speaking to a small roomful of people but discovered that the talk would be also be going out on Web Air. I was afraid and asked my personal Angel CB to help me. In fact I said: "Please will *you* do it" and pulled myself out of the way and just channeled directly what she told me. Thank God all went well and the talk was a success. But I forgot to take my mobile phone out of my pocket. I discovered that Angels don't always mix well with electrical equipment. My mobile behaved strangely for the next 24 hours; it wouldn't allow me to make any calls and when I put it down it literally hopped about on its own.

Friends who were present at the talk witnessed the phone's behavior and were amazed. I stayed with friends in Palmers Green that evening. I can still recollect the look on their son Sam's face as the phone danced on its own across the coffee table. Finally I sent healing to the phone and in desperation I asked CB if she could calm the phone down, as I needed to use it. I was heard. The phone readjusted overnight; by the next day it was back to normal. I have an iPhone; it is pretty stable usually. This behavior was a complete aberration, and it has not behaved in this way since. But that is not surprising, as I have now learnt to take my mobile out of my pocket before asking for CB to assist me.

Chapter Ten

I like this quote for its clarity and simplicity, taken from the physics.org website.

We are all made of stardust. It sounds like a line from a poem, but there is some solid science behind this statement too: almost every element on Earth was formed at the heart of a star. Next time you're out gazing at stars twinkling in the night sky, spare a thought for the tumultuous reactions they play host to. It's easy to forget that stars owe their light to the energy released by nuclear fusion reactions at their cores. These are the very same reactions which created chemical elements like carbon or iron, the building blocks, which make up the world around us. After the Big Bang, tiny particles bound together to form hydrogen and helium. As time went on, young stars formed when clouds of gas and dust gathered under the effect of gravity, heating up as they became denser. At the stars' cores, bathed in temperatures of over 10 million degrees C, hydrogen and then helium nuclei fused to form heavier elements. A reaction known as nucleosynthesis. This reaction continues in stars today as lighter elements are converted into heavier ones. Relatively young stars like our Sun convert hydrogen to produce helium, just like the first stars of our universe. Once they run out of hydrogen, they begin to transform helium into beryllium and carbon. As these heavier nuclei are produced, they too are burnt inside stars to synthesize heavier and heavier elements. Different sized stars play host to different fusion reactions, eventually forming everything from oxygen to iron. During a supernova, when a massive star explodes at the end of its life, the resulting high-energy environment enables the creation of some of the heaviest elements including iron and nickel. The explosion

also disperses the different elements across the universe, scattering the stardust, which now makes up planets including Earth.
– www.physics.org[9]

It was through the realization that we all contain stardust that I was further supported in being able to connect with my own personal Angel, CB, and carry out healing. The insight helped me to value myself and realize that if I had stars within me then I was of value, that I was worth the effort of putting time aside to undertake my own personal spiritual journey. There were patterns of behavior that I wanted to break and I wanted to understand myself more fully so that I could be happier, and also so that I could be more effective when working with clients. In particular, I sought to understand our world and its place in the cosmos from a view of appreciation and wonder. I also came to realize that due to the fact humans are energetic beings we have the capacity to hold within our being all of our experiences, good and bad. I find this to be remarkable.

When I channel CB she often says: "Pinch your skin and marvel at the Divinity within." I see how perfectly we are integrated with both the Earth and the Cosmos. Dan Kahn my Bi-Aura tutor taught me: "Look at yourself, you are a miracle."

It is helpful to keep this deep knowledge of our interconnect-edness at the forefront of my mind as it assists me in understanding and being able to use energy healing. After all, I am part of the universe and there is no reason why I, or anyone else, cannot know the secrets of the universe and tap into the unlimited cosmic energy or Earth energy to help heal others and ourselves.

Chapter Eleven

In my journey of self-realization I investigated several disciplines and therapeutic techniques. These included astrology and Past Life Regression.

In Totnes in Devon, I had my chart read by a local astrologer. She looked at my chart and said that she was almost certain that I had been in service as a healer in a past life. She told me:

> Neptune in the 10th house shows you will be honored for your spiritual gifts, as it is the apex of the fabulous kite. The kite sits on an amazing grand trine (3 planets aligned in a triangle at 60 degrees), an exact one with Jupiter in the 12th house (esoteric mysteries) trine power house Pluto, trine your 3rd house sun. It's truly magnificent! This should boost your confidence. You will do what you intend and all will come good! Venus in 2nd will ultimately bring the rewards.

At the time, I found this astrological reading helpful to me for its insight and validation. On receiving clear instruction and direction from my personal Angel in 2010, I was then able to use this astrological information as a mechanism for empowerment, to move forward rather than stand still and to understand myself better and to equip myself to live in this world and to take up my service at Watkins Books and with my private clients, and to write this book.

I find spiritual readings very helpful; they help me realign my efforts and energy. This particular astrological reading five years ago showed me areas of weakness and of strength. The fact that my chart also indicated that I have the capacity to connect with the spiritual world gave me a boost of confidence at a time when I was experiencing a lack of faith in myself and my psychic abilities. Past Life Regression Therapy also helped me to accept my psychic attributes; I found this experience to be most profound. By seeing how I operated in a past life I was able to understand, forgive and rectify myself for mistakes that I had made in this lifetime.

There were definitely certain past life traits and perspectives that I had brought in with me to this lifetime. In the regressed life in Assyria, I had been Melissa, a priestess. This explained exactly why I always thought that I should live in a large house, and my lack of understanding about how money works. It also clearly explains why in this lifetime I can access Divine energy and I have a capacity for spirituality. Accepting myself as a future incarnation of 'Melissa' has helped me to accept and channel CB. But Past Life Regression is not for the fainthearted; please research this treatment thoroughly and consider the process thoughtfully before undertaking training or a session with a certified teacher.

I went to a Past Life Therapist whom I felt great trust for but I was still completely terrified with the prospect of the process. Afterwards just listening to the recording of the session frightened me, but it was an invaluable experience; it gave me great personal insight. But I have to be honest, it did take me a good month to recover from my Past Life Regression treatment; I have not mustered up the courage to go back. The prospect of having had – and perhaps reliving – a violent death is high, therefore I am not keen to enter such a situation however trained the therapist.

During the Past Life Regression you 'relive' with guiding imagery and professional support past events and the emotions that rise from the experiences. You then need to return to normal life and integrate the knowledge you gained. It is quite a journey and not one I am rushing to do again; even though I hope I do. My session did alert me to a tendency I have that I have since worked on: my tendency to act as though I am a Goddess. Yes, I am not too proud to admit I used to veer to arrogance at times and distance myself from people in day-to-day life due to this expression in my ego. I have since worked on grounding my soul and my behavior.

After my one and only Past Life Regression session in 2011, I received by chance a real life validation that the Priestess known as Melissae had once existed.

Two weeks after my session, a friend who knew I had undertaken Past Life Regression was stung by a bee. That day she also happened to see a copy of *Kindred Spirit Magazine* which contained an article on bees. This article mentioned 'Melissae' and told how they were priestesses with the responsibility for accessing the Divine. Priestesses at Cybele's Temples in Asia Minor, Greece, and Rome were called Melissai or Melissae, the Greek and Latin words for bees. Bees have an ancient reputation as the bringers of order; their hives served as models for organizing temples in many Mediterranean cultures. These priestesses were often prophets or oracles who entered an ecstatic trance induced by preparations that included ingesting honey. The Greek word for this state of transfigured consciousness is *Enthusiasmos*, 'within is a God', the root of our word enthusiasm.[10]

Chapter Twelve

I first came across the process of Radical Forgiveness in 2009 at a New Year's Day party on Dartmoor, Devon, England. When someone at a party talked about it to me for the first time, I felt the room tilt and lurch; I had an immediate spiritual connection and reaction to the term. So I knew what to do next! At the time, I was harboring a lot of latent anger towards my former husband. Radical Forgiveness Treatment helped me extract the anger I had accumulated and replace it with feelings of profound compassion, universality and understanding.

Radical Forgiveness is a spiritual intelligence technique introduced by Colin Tipping; he is a worldwide workshop leader who works both in America and the UK. Radical Forgiveness is something infinitely greater, more all encompassing and more revolutionary than conventional forgiveness. It breaks down into 5 distinct stages, the first three of which are more or less the same as in conventional forgiveness. It's at Stage 4 that it gets to be exciting and, for many of us, quite challenging. Colin Tipping has given permission for the Radical Forgiveness process to be outlined here; a trained facilitator is recommended to guide you in the initial stages of orientation.

Stage 1: Telling the Story. This is where you tell the story of what happened, why you feel victimized, who is to blame and so on. The goal is to have your story witnessed and validated.

Stage 2: Feeling the Feelings. This is where you give yourself permission to feel the full range of feelings associated with the story, no matter what they are.

Stage 3: Collapsing the Story. In this part you take a step backwards and try to understand the person's motives for doing what they did, bring some empathy, mercy and compassion into the mix, and try to cut them some slack in spite of what they did to you. You also try to cut out all the stuff that isn't quite true but you added to the story to make it seem more than it was, and so on. But this is as far as conventional forgiveness can go. It still identifies you as a victim, and even though you are making an effort to forgive the person, he or she is not let off the hook. He/she is still seen as the perpetrator and responsible for your unhappiness.

Stage 4: Reframing the Story. It's at this point that Radical Forgiveness takes us where conventional forgiveness can never go and where few of us have ever been before. But it is the key to a whole new way of thinking. It asks that we make a dramatic shift in our perception of ourselves and the world we inhabit. In the reframe, we are asked to become willing to embrace the idea that there is Divine purpose in everything and that there are no mistakes. It's where we begin to see that at the spiritual level there is nothing to forgive because everything that occurs happens not TO us but FOR us. Even though we don't know what they are, there are reasons why we choose the experiences we create and this applies to everything that happens. It is all part of the Divine plan for our lives, and we created it all. It's our own Divine plan playing itself out and there are no exceptions. We no longer ask, "How to forgive?" Your rational mind will say it's crazy, but your Higher Self, with its own form of intelligence – Spiritual Intelligence – knows the truth and totally gets it. So don't worry – it works anyway.

Stage 5: Integrating the New Story. The old victim story lived in every cell of our body. Having dissolved that story, the new (reframed) story has to be put in its place. For that to happen we need to do something physical for the integration to take place. It can be achieved through writing, speaking it out, dancing, music and, best of all, breath work. People who try Radical Forgiveness become profoundly changed. All their old hurts dissolve. Their long-held resentments seem to just melt away. Relationships are healed. Connections get made and synchronicities occur that show that there is a different set of laws operating at some other level. Problems simply go away and life just works better.

Summary: The practical aspects of Radical Forgiveness are as follows:

a) It requires no skill or special ability. Anyone can do it, even if they are totally skeptical – it still works. One does not even have to believe in its central idea that there are no accidents and that our soul has created the circumstances of our lives for our spiritual growth. All it requires is a willingness to at least be open to that possibility.

b) Since it works energetically, it operates outside of the parameters of time and space. Consequently, results are immediate and distance is no factor in terms of the effect it might have energetically on all the people involved, as well as on the actual situation causing the initial upset.

c) There is no inherent conflict between the need to condemn and the desire to forgive, because from a spiritual perspective nothing wrong has happened and there is nothing to forgive.

d) It sets one free from victim consciousness. From a spiritual perspective, there are no victims and perpetrators – just teachers and learners.

Because I find Radical Forgiveness to be so helpful I asked Celestial Bell about it. I can't capture all of her response here because there are concepts that I cannot understand and put into words. I receive impressions mostly about a stretching of consciousness and a humming sound. However, the essence of it suggests that Radical Forgiveness is a mechanism to lift the human soul to the Angelic realm and vibration, allowing access to Divine love and forgiveness. Because it enables humans to tune in to the Angelic frequency, Angelic intervention, assistance and healing are accessed at will. The Radical Forgiveness technique enables humans to release pain and to be able to 'flip' instantly into another dimension and live their lives within a higher spiritual framework. I understand and have frequently seen Angels that are always present at such healing.

I also got a sense of Angelic gratitude to Colin Tipping for his tenacity and deep holding of the concept. The feeling is that Angels are pleased that his methodology of healing at a spiritual level has been honored; that it is authentic and that he has promoted it tirelessly. It seems the Angels have granted him an 'Angel Warrant': they are very pleased Colin Tipping is helping us humans through this technique, therefore the Angels thus far have blessed all his efforts.

It seems to me that episodes of pain are a bit like the seaweed that I used to pop when I was a child. They get embedded into the energy field and prevent living fully, but once they are brought to light and popped or dissolved, away they go never to be seen again and are replaced by the ability to be and live in the moment and have cleaner and projection-free relationships, infinitely more joyous than loaded interactions.

There is another technique, which I use a great deal, both with my clients and with myself. This method is particularly helpful in dissolving pain and taking it out of the body or etheric field. Burdens that have been stored are then removed. Often in a completely miraculous way. The technique is called the *Ho'oponopono* prayer: the Hawaiian Code of Reconciliation and Forgiveness. I use my own adapted version of the technique as described by Barbel Mohr in *Cosmic Ordering: The Next Step*.[11]

This is how it works.

In brief, I work to identify any issue that has upset either my client or myself and why. Often I ask CB to help me intuit extra reasons that may have been overlooked or forgotten. Then my client takes (or I take) a crystal in one hand and very solemnly reads each issue out loud; and after everyone recites *Ho'oponopono*:

I am Sorry, I Forgive You, and I Love You, Thank You.

I see these as words of unmaking: They represent a powerful mantra that helps to take away emotion, projections and pain.

Chapter Thirteen

In Totnes in 2013, I attended my first Shiva Shakti Dance Class run by Boe Huntress,[12] an experienced and talented Shakti teacher and songwriter.

Shiva Shakti originates in India. I didn't read up on this form of dance before I took the class; I just showed up knowing nothing because I felt drawn to the information on the poster in our community. The dances we did that day impacted upon me as they were designed to do.

In the dance of the Warrior I immediately saw how small I had been making myself, on an emotional and spiritual plane. We were invited to see ourselves as if we were a spirit. While I was dancing the Warrior I glimpsed my soul light in its entirety and realized that I have a large presence. By keeping myself small – hidden away and not undertaking any public service – I was not serving anyone and not developing my true spiritual and emotional potential. The dance gave me the permission to be myself; to release my true spirit into the world and let it do its work.

Shiva Shakti Movement Meditation: The Shiva Shakti Dance is an ancient women's movement meditation that has been passed down through the female yoginis of India. It is a form of embodied meditation that allows the dancer to travel into the right-brain hemisphere where processes are more intuitive, holistic and creative. The focus is on felt sensation in the body, particularly opening to sensation in the lower half of the body, which has often been disconnected due to the taboo nature of female sexuality, to experiences of sexual shock or simply to excess focus on rational mind and the left-brain hemisphere.

The dance works with the principle that every atom and molecule in the universe is dancing and spiraling. In this sense it's a very natural movement with no steps to learn. There is a basic stance and form. The movement works to undo the diverting conditioning of control and rigidity in our bodies. It is called Shiva Shakti Dance because it embraces the union between Spirit (Shiva) and matter (Shakti), formless and form. In the Hindu tradition Shiva and Shakti are the Divine masculine and Divine feminine principles of creative power that together create reality.

The Shiva Shakti Dance is founded upon the understanding that the center of a woman's power lies in her womb and is conducted through the opening to her womb. Historically, this has been a feared and suppressed place of female sensuality. Within the dance, the focus is on sensation and pleasure as a source of connection to oneself.

Once the dancer has been dancing for ten to twenty minutes – or sooner, depending on her level of attention and familiarity with the dance – she will begin to transition into the right hemisphere of the brain. This is the nonlinear side of the brain, which communicates in images and pictures, similar to the dream state. It is a powerful place of depth within oneself from which to receive guidance.

The right side of the brain is our emotional intelligence, and as we make the transition from the left brain, we may encounter a number of unfelt feelings that have been stored in the body. The movement and attention in this dance acts to uncoil anything that is in contraction or held tightly within the body, and we use our bodies to conduct and ground whatever is moving.

From the right brain our essential nature, or self, is experienced as exceptionally different from the beliefs and notions that we might hold about ourselves from a perspective of critical judgment. In the dance we distinguish between this essential self and what we call the wounded self, which comes from cultural conditioning and life experiences that have been used to create our identities.

The idea of the Shiva Shakti Dance is to associate one's identity with the essential self, who is embodied and rooted in the present moment, rather than the wounded self. The dance is a practice that can help access this sense of self and presence more generally in life. (Source: Boe Huntress.)

Chapter Fourteen

Our deepest fear is not that we are inadequate. Our deepest fear is that we are powerful beyond measure. It is our light not our darkness that most frightens us. We ask ourselves: Who am I to be brilliant, gorgeous, talented, and fabulous? Actually, who are you not to be? You are a child of God. Your playing small does not serve the world. There is nothing enlightened about shrinking so that other people won't feel insecure around you. We are all meant to shine, as children do. We were born to make manifest the glory of God that is within us. It's not just in some of us; it's in everyone. And as we let our own light shine, we unconsciously give other people permission to do the same. As we are liberated from our own fear, our presence automatically liberates others.

– Marianne Williamson

This widely known and much loved quote of Marianne Williamson is taken from her book *A Return to Love: Reflections on the Principles of a Course in Miracles.*[13]

I was inspired from the moment that I heard these particular words while taking a training course for my local government work in 1995; it gave me an *Aha* moment and I shifted my perception. From that moment, I have placed the concept of having the right and the ability to shine as a unique individual in the world at the center of my work, whether it was as a healer, a writer or coach; whether I was working on myself or facilitating the shining of others. The quote also resonated with some Jewish teachings that provide a heartbeat to my work and which I consider to be important in assisting humans to make 'The Great Shift' I speak of (in the Preface on page 1) that CB so often mentions when I channel her.

One teaching was these wise words from Rabbi Hillel, the renowned Jewish Sage and Philosopher who was born in

Babylonia in the first century BCE. Rabbi Hillel was asked to sum up the entire Torah while 'standing on one foot'. He said: "Whatever you don't like, don't do to others. The rest of the Torah is the explanation of this statement. Go study it."

'Don't do to others what is hateful to yourself' is the summary in *Gemara Shabbos*, another source in the Jewish writings. How different the world would be if everyone living on our planet upheld this human ethic.

Another Jewish teaching that resonates with me regarding our right as humans to be fully present in the world and to contribute in our own unique way is one that was taught to me by my friend Thena who is a rabbi's daughter. She taught me: "One of the main principles of *Chasidic* Judaism is to serve God in happiness, with joy, with *Simcha* (Hebrew translation) as it says in Psalm 100: Serve Hashem (one of the Jewish names for God) with happiness, come before Him in joyous song." Another Jewish *principle* that I hold close to my heart as someone that believes in God and the wonder of the Divine is that our present life is a rectification for our past life; that in this lifetime we may have to endure or undertake certain tasks or overcome particular challenges to rectify, or make good things we did wrong or incorrectly or in ignorance in our past time; we have to make a *Tikkun* (the Hebrew word for rectification) in this lifetime. Past Life Regression work can help a person with the work of *Tikkunim*. It is through this work that we can repair any wrong accountable to us from our former life; in doing we make a correction in the world today; we change for the good the possibilities in our own lives.

How can one be joyful in a world when there is also rectification work to be done? It is through joy that we come to know we are given the opportunity to repent and start over. This is the power of joy and forgiveness in our own lives and in the world around us. This is the task of every human being and whatever we do we cannot avoid it; in some form or another God will bring the work we need to do to us and we will be asked or prompted or sometimes, I am sorry to say, be forced do to the work we were brought into this world to do. If we can do 'this work' with joy, all the better for us and all the better for the world. For a world with joy and song, as we do the work we were brought into this world to do, has got to be a brighter, better world.

In Part Three of this book I write about how extraordinary my life became once I began to ask for Angelic help with the work I believe God prompts me to do in this world. When I mention manifestation and abundance I am not necessarily referring to material things. The more that I walk on my conscious spiritual journey as I live my life in this lifetime the less I focus upon money as an objective (not that I spurn it). Instead, I am looking for serenity, freedom and connectedness; to be able to partake in the repair of the world; realignment; and for my own inner richness in the process of my own rectification of self – while I help others on their journey.

As I work through my day doing my holy work I have a prayer in mind from *Forms of Prayer for Jewish Worship* by the Assembly of Reform Rabbis Great Britain;[14] it is a prayer that augments my own personal, spiritual, transformative socioeconomic and environmental worldview. I have partially but not wholly been influenced through the economics of transition and Deep Ecology taught by the Schumacher College in Dartington, Devon.[15] The prayer encapsulates my hope for the world:

Therefore, Lord our God, we put our hope in You. Soon let us witness the glory of Your power; when the worship of material things shall pass away from the earth, and prejudice and superstition shall at last be cut off; when the world will be set right by the rule of God and all mankind shall speak out in your name and all the wicked of the Earth shall turn to You. Then all who inhabit this world shall meet in under-standing, and shall know that to You alone each one shall submit, and pledge himself in every tongue. In Your presence Lord our God they shall bow down and be humble, honoring the glory of Your being. All shall accept the duty of building Your kingdom so that Your reign of goodness shall come soon and last forever. For Yours alone is the true kingdom, and only the glory of Your rule endures forever. So it is written in Your Torah: "The Lord shall rule forever and ever", so it is prophesied: The Lord shall be as a king over all the earth. On that day the Lord shall be One and known as One.

I add a footnote to this prayer. This prayer does not expect anyone to convert to any religion; for me it is about respecting the faith of each person in the universe whatever that may be. Try asking a roomful of a hundred people for their definition of God; there would I believe be a hundred different answers. In the case of this prayer when I read the word God I conjure up the Divine. I see the Divine in the same way as I see Angels as neither masculine nor feminine. For me, God or the Divine is an energy outside of the human split of male and female and "Just is everything and limitless and all knowing and all being and is everything."

I am comfortable within Judaism; as a woman it is where I am most at ease. This is my own personal interpretation and what I am drawn to. The Jewish calendar of the year follows a lunar cycle; this means that every year festivals take place at different times to that of the Solar cycle that we follow mechanically year in and year out. I like that Judaism is an agricultural religion with a close connection to the Earth. I like having my place as a woman within the home and being able to light candles every Friday to say thank you for my week. I see evidence that women are honored in Judaism. Each Friday night on the Jewish Shabbat one of my friends' husband sings to her, telling her that she is more precious than pearls (Proverbs 3:1).

Although many of my friends and I notice and rail against

sexism within Judaism, it is a sexism which many women rail against manifested in the mainstream world. Judaism has had to fight for its survival within a dominant culture where it has been mandatory often by force to recognize and worship the dominant and rational masculine. My belief is that this is an aberration and a drifting away from the core of Judaism, which at its center honors the feminine and the masculine, equally.

The prayer offers me hope that I have the capacity to be able to draw back my more selfish impulses; to slow down and put the needs of the Earth first. While I often do not succeed in living such a life of grace, I am committed to trying to put energy into *Tikkun Olam*, or the repair of the world, into the realignment and adjustment that I perceive is helping to raise the vibration of the Earth. And I know that in this I am not alone. I am one of many men and women, young people and children engaged in the same adventure.

Chapter Fifteen

In the spring of 2010 my marriage came to its natural end; it was not that anything specific happened, we grew apart. Neither of us was unfaithful to the other. Our marriage just ran out of energy and it was not possible to reignite it. We both wanted different things and to journey in different directions. At the time we separated we were both very angry with each other, but over the last five years things settled down and we now maintain a respectful and peaceful friendship. Although we have gone our separate ways I still care about Steven and he cares about me. He is in a solid new relationship now with a woman who suits him. I am pleased for him and have no attachment. It is good to see him so happy.

Post-separation and divorce, while I explored and discovered new ways to augment my journey to spiritual enlightenment and service, I encountered a new challenge: how to navigate new male relationships as a mature woman, not a position I imagined myself to return to when I married in 1988. As with all new experiences, I have learned from my mistakes which a friend recently reframed for me: "There are no mistakes, Wendy, just life lessons. You are enrolled in Earth School… Go vita; onwards!" The lessons that I learned came when I was caught up in an episode of unrequited love.

This is a book about Angels and I only mention this episode of unrequited love in passing because of the opportunities that it gave me to learn about myself and heal. In turn this helped me to draw my ego back and to become a better conduit for CB.

In her book *Wild Love*, Gill Edwards[16] speaks about her own episode of unrequited love. *Wild Love* is a complex book; one that I highly recommend. There is not space to discuss it in depth here nor is it appropriate; but in relation to my situation page 261 offered me insight:

In any relationship, you will tend to go into Sacrifice if you feel 'not good enough' for the Other, or if you have less power, money, education or social status, or if you have more feminine energy (that is, you are more emotional, intuitive and relationship orientated). If you have stronger masculine energy (which doesn't necessarily mean being male, but being more left brained, logical, assertive or competitive than the Other, you will tend to go into Control. And whenever you slip into Control-Sacrifice, you are both in ego and the relationship becomes dysfunctional.

What can prevent a relationship (or any personal inter-action) spiraling down into ego-based patterns?

- Firstly the presence of unconditional love – which sees everyone as good, which makes no judgment, and which sees no inequality, no power differences; a love which sees the Other as equal in every way. (The ego readily labels others as 'better than' or 'less than' oneself, whereas the deep Self is blind to inequality. Whether it sees a street urchin or a princess, a monk or a mass murderer, it sees only Source energy expressing itself – or being resisted – in a myriad different forms.)
- Secondly, the utter commitment to trusting your emotional guidance – the God within – so that you stay connected to Source energy and take 100% responsibility for your own experience and feelings.

In other words, what heals any relationship is wild love connecting to your deep Self. Without the deep self, without the divine feminine there is only tame love.

Releasing myself from the entrapment of unrequited love was not easy. In the end I went 'cold turkey'. I put the time aside to mourn. As well as mourning my unrequited love, at the same time I realized that I had somehow bypassed mourning my lost marriage properly so I put time into that too, realizing how much Steven had meant to me and how I missed his care and holding. I took full responsibility for my part in the separation and the pain that it had caused our sons. I took myself out of circulation. The universe helpfully arranged this during the time that I went back from London to Paignton in Devon, a small seaside town just over the hill from Totnes: I talk about how this occurred in Part Three, Chapter 10.

I refused all social occasions although I had invitations to parties. I allowed myself to really feel my feelings and just do what my body wished me to do. I spent a lot of time sleeping, a lot of time crying. When I was angry I did more clearing via radical forgiveness and *Ho'oponopono*. There were times in which I frightened myself. On one occasion I cried so much for three hours, I thought that I would not be able to stop. The tears just kept on flowing and flowing. In the end I decided not to try and stop them but to just let them flow. The pain during this time was so great that once more I couldn't walk down the road without the help of my Silver Rope to pull me along. You know what – aged 55 and not used since I was 15, I needed it again and there it was. To walk out of the door and go to the shops and buy food, I had to ask the Rope: "Take me to that tree." "Now to that next tree; or that lamppost." Somehow I got along. Eventually my misery shifted.

All of this may sound self-indulgent to you but I am glad that I invested this time in myself to really feel my feelings. The worst of the grief came, not when I was angry with others or in victim mode, but when I turned and faced myself. I saw how the consequences to my actions had impacted on other people, on those whom I love, in particular my children; but also my ex-husband and friends. I saw how I wasn't always that kind to my unrequited love, had hurt and drawn down on him too. It was hard, painful work to realize and integrate my sorrows and my shadow.

One day I woke up without thinking about unrequited love or my lost marriage, or my fears and regrets. I got out of my bed. There was no heaviness and no weight. I looked out of the door and saw that the world is beautiful and that I need not be afraid. It was all manageable; not only was it all manageable but I was and am loved. I slipped back into my work.

I had embarked on a new career; and if I wanted to be a highly effective and happy Angel Reader, Energy Healer and Intuitive Coach it was imperative that I focus on the work in hand: training, seeing clients and finishing this book!

Celestial Bell was insistent: "One of your main tasks is to assist with the realignment of the Earth. The spiritual becomes material and the material becomes spiritual."

When I asked for more specific clarification on this task, CB replied: "Every moment the vibration of the Earth changes; the material becomes spiritual; the spiritual becomes material. The feminine and masculine integrate and evolve."

I had a glimpse of how this lesson might be realized in the life of men and women; that there is not just one way, the man's way or the woman's way; no such way exists anymore. Man and woman exist in man, and man and woman exist in woman.

From this I understood her to mean that there was too great a polarization between the feminine and masculine roles in our society. Men had been taught to deny the feminine and compassionate aspect of themselves, and women had often internalized a distorted view of the masculine, which disconnected them from their power to be effective in the world. CB gave me a further insightful vision: I saw very clearly that the disconnect between men and women had a lot to answer for. It has very directly impacted upon the way in which we relate to the Earth: discounting the Earth's balance; crassly taking what we want rather than just that which we can carry ourselves, which is what animals do. Apart from squirrels, as far as I know it is only humans who take and hoard.

CB continued to show me that conflict between the sexes must stop if we are to be able to be integrated human beings; fully in our power, fully honoring and respecting one another. This means that there is no more time for a battle between the sexes. We are better served by working as one; in unity for the common good but above for the self-actualization of each other, man and woman. The conflict and challenge of this generation and beyond is the shortsightedness of man and woman. By uniting and making the best of our attributes we will be able to thrive and create and love and heal the planet.

Put simply, no more perception that Men are from Mars and Women are from Venus. There is an urgent need for the masculine and feminine energy to cooperate and to integrate; to enter into a new dialogue with each other for the benefit of today and future generations with regard to our roles, our responsibilities and obligations to each other and the universe. In other words CB is trying to advise that as humans we cease the blaming, shaming and taming power games that Gill Edwards speaks of and instead move into the state of *Wild Love*. This is an unconditional love based on freedom and responsibility rather than a codependent dynamic that is based on the exercise of power and upon fear.

I definitely had my work cut out for me if I was going to deal with any of these objectives and targets on any level; mostly because I believed my Angel and her vision, a vision that made sense to me and inspired me. But processing all of this was not easy. It's all very well for CB to send me visions, stretching new ways of relating; but sometimes the challenge of translating these visions into intelligent and useful communication felt beyond my capacity. And I had questions. What did CB really mean and what could I really do to help realize this vision?

Imagine my surprise and delight when I stumbled across the teachings of the eminent psychotherapist Carl Jung who had comprehensively explored the very vision outlined by my very own personal Angel in 2012, similar concepts and a theoretical framework for understanding and pragmatic application. Did I stumble onto the answers to the nagging questions surrounding my lifework; I am not sure. Let us say CB engineered me to be in the right place at the right time to receive some right answers, and which prompted me to think of a way forward for myself to assist with the realignment of mankind with my own spiritual contribution and service!

Watkins Books in Central London often hosts talks with authors. One day, shortly after CB reminded me of one of the main purposes of my new lifework, I got delayed at work and stayed to listen to a talk by Claire Dunne. Claire was introducing her new book *Carl Jung: Wounded Healer of the Soul, an Illustrated Biography*.[17]

Claire Dunne is an author and broadcaster/producer in radio and television. She was born in Ireland but has been based for many years in Australia. Claire is tall, slender, dignified; has a beauty, calmness, grace about her; a generosity that I liked. She was very careful to say that she came to Jung as an ordinary reading member of the public. Claire told of her fascination with Jung and her hope that her 'naïve' exploration would bring him to a wider audience. Jung lived 26.7.1875–6.6.1961. Jung was a contemporary and close friend of Freud. But unlike Freud he placed the human psyche within the context of a spiritual world and a world that was full of synchronicity and order. This worldview impacted on him as it meant a fall from grace for Jung: he argued with Freud and was estranged from him for many years. As a man operating in a highly scientific, rational milieu he was ostracized and his professional standing challenged. For some years he was ridiculed and placed in professional isolation. All for recognizing that we live in a Divine and synchronistic universe.

You can imagine why when hearing all of this I felt that I had entered Heaven. Finally everything began to make sense. I felt validated by hearing what had happened to Jung once he had begun to be open about his affinity to God and the Divine. This has been my struggle too. Perhaps it is everyone's struggle.

Claire was also able to bring clarity to a subject most puzzling to me. She spoke about Carl Jung's theory on the process of individ-ualization; the integration of the shadow; the integration of the masculine, which Jung called the *anima*, and feminine, which Jung called the *animus* aspect within us all.

After the author talk, Claire Dunne hosted a discussion with Watkins Books customers. I joined the dialogue. Because I had been struggling to articulate the channeled messages which I had from CB, I asked Claire if she knew what happens to a person when they integrate the masculine and feminine, and their shadow? Without hesitation Claire replied: "They obtain immanence."

CB has been very clear in terms of my task: the purpose of this book is to bring inspiration and comfort during 'The Great Shift'. I am no expert on Jung, or Freud. When I am in Watkins I am surrounded by heaps and heaps of books written by people who are experts in these fields. You the Reader have access to all of these books; I am not needed in this realm, except perhaps to facilitate access to the concept of immanence.

But on that day, far from answering my question, Claire's answer left me more perplexed than ever. Now I wondered, why was CB so insistent that the way to immanence lay in the integration of the spiritual and the material? For what reason did the masculine and feminine need to integrate? If the outcome were to be that we step into a world that exists on a higher vibra-tional plane how would this world look? And what is meant by immanence?

The bookshop audience group began to explore these

concepts and I realized why I had struggled so much. It's because it is so hard to put into words. We all grappled and stumbled that evening in Watkins, bandying the words 'Jung', 'Freud' and 'immanence' backwards and forwards between ourselves until it was time for Claire to complete her book signings and for us all to go home. I was still none the wiser in terms of achieving a definition of immanence.

Because I enjoyed the discussion so much I bought a copy of *Carl Jung: Wounded Healer of the Soul, an Illustrated Biography*. I saw that Jung was exploring the concepts of integration of the masculine and feminine and of God and of the Divine. Claire's book, *Wounded Healer of the Soul*, includes a lot of original material. Reading the actual words of Jung, I found it interesting to note the density of the language and the genius of the articulation. Even if I am not a Jungian or Freudian expert, or a psychologist, Jung's writing has so much authenticity that I realized he is truly able to provide insight to the human soul.

But although I was grateful for the illumination I was still on my quest: I did not yet have a definition of the word immanence nor a way to put it into words that could explain to you the Reader clearly what this core message of CB meant in actuality, and what its impact might be should it be realized.

Chapter Sixteen

It was my son Zachary who guided me on the next stage of my Quest to find out and define the meaning of immanence and its implications. Zack has a curious mind, and is an intellectual; sometimes I can't keep up with him. Zack likes business lectures and is an avid follower of TEDTalks (www.ted.com), a great venue online and through seminars all over the world for anyone looking to be inspired and informed by this generation's Great Thinkers and Inventors.

With his intellect Zack can be very forceful and now he was being insistent: Perhaps he was prompted by CB? I don't know.

"Mum, I have sent you a great talk by Simon Sinek, on TED. Will you watch it?"

"Maybe later when I am not so busy?"

"MUM, I HAVE SENT YOU A GREAT TALK…"

"OK, I will watch it!" I settled down at my computer and clicked on the link that Zack had sent over three weeks earlier.

Simon Sinek's TEDTalk was entitled: "How great leaders inspire action". What I found intriguing and fascinating about Sinek's eighteen-minute talk is he gave a biological-led response not a psychological explanation to explain the capacity of great leaders to inspire. I was glad that I had listened to Zack; or rather that Zack had guided me. Simon's talk added a further piece of the puzzle to my understanding of the concept of immanence. Because I think that it might add to your understanding I have also transcribed the gist of the talk below, although you could watch it if you like:[18]

Simon Sinek codified the capacity for inspired leadership and inspired products; he has developed a model called "The Golden Circle". He suggests that organizations such as Apple and great leaders such as Dr. Martin Luther King are successful because they "think, act and communicate from inside out". They tell people why they are doing something not how they are doing something. Sinek states that people do not buy what you do, they buy why you do it; you have to give a person a reason to buy or do something. You have to inspire and persuade them; when they are inspired or persuaded they will then take action. His "Golden Circle" principle corresponds directly to the three major components of our brain from top down. The outer section of the brain is the homo sapien brain – the neocortex – and this is the newest section that is responsible for language and rationality. The two sections in the middle correspond to the why and how, the limbic sections. Here resides our capacity for feeling, for trust, loyalty, for decision making and all human behavior. This part of the brain has no capacity for language; it is responsible for 'gut decisions'; is lead by the heart and soul; the emotion and spiritual needs of man. The limbic sections need to know why to do something before they decide to take action.

Sinek said, Dr. Martin Luther King was able to attract "250,000 people… on the Mall in Washington" in the summer of 1963 because he believed that there are two types of laws in the world, the laws that are made by man and the laws that are made by a higher authority, and it is only when the two coincide that we will live in a just world. Dr. King gave an 'I have a dream' speech, not an 'I have a plan' speech. In other words people were inspired to blood, sweat and tears by dreams, not by rationality.

The connection between Simon Sinek and immanence may seem obscure to you the Reader. Perhaps it may look as if I have gone off on a tangent; but for me this talk sent light bulbs flashing in my head. No wonder I couldn't find the words for immanence. There are no words. Perhaps Immanence does not relate to the rational mind at all. It is a feeling. And as the concept of God is understood differently by individuals and societies, perhaps this also applies to the concept of immanence?

Soon after watching Simon's talk, another scholar gave additional insight. The following quote is by Jenna Lilla.[19]

To open to immanence is to be connected to that which is greater than ourselves: to feel the flow of life, to be enlivened by the divinity, which is all around us and within us. Although we cannot directly speak of immanence, poetry and art often emanate from its depths. For it is in the depths of our being that we discover the truth manifesting itself in our hearts yearning to come into a deeper relationship with the divine as it permeates life.

This process of coming into a deeper relationship with life is a process of coming into relationship with the 'deep truth'. It is interrelationship that is both with ourselves and with the world around us. It is a discovery, an immanent turn, available to those who have searched and found their 'individuality'. It is a shift of focus from individuation to interrelation: from me to we. And thus immanence is love, but not libidinal love as desire. Instead, it is divine love, love for life, and love for being.

– Jenna Lilla

Sometimes I am so frustrated by myself! How could it be that it took so long for the penny to drop? Poor CB, she had to be immeasurably patient with me. Of course Angels would like us to integrate the material and the spiritual and the masculine and feminine: they are working with us to have Heaven on Earth, to be in Nirvana, to be in Bliss. To be entirely unto ourselves; in perfect balance. We are so immeasurably dear to Angels; they would like us to live to our highest vibration and to access all that is good on Earth. To shine; to be complete.

I stretched my consciousness to CB; I felt that there was amusement emanating from her as well as a feeling of the deepest love. I heard her say, "You are nearly there; bring together all that you know."

Going near such grandeur reduced me to a child again. Humbled I went back to my Quest. Now I kept thinking about childhood and Pooh Bear! You know when he sat and pondered for a little bit and thought and thought! I went through that process. I thought and I thought. Eventually I wondered, what do Angels think of us humans? Really and truly? What did they want from us? We have such a big task. We are custodians of the Planet Earth. It's a huge responsibility.

I asked CB, "What do you Angels think of us Humans?" Once again CB seemed amused. She patiently replied, "You are the Divine made Manifest: The living embodiment of God." And then I understood.

I realized that I had known the answer all along. I had partially been taught it on the Bi-Aura Energy Course and in all of my research since then. My understanding is thus.

We are spiritual beings having a human experience: We are creatures of the universe. We contain the same amount of water and matter within us as the surface of the world. Our energetic frequency is the same as that of the world. We contain stardust. Each and every one of us is a miracle. We each act as a living conductor: we manifest God through making the spiritual material. We use our bodies to do this. Everything that we conceptualize and produce has to travel through the human body via each Chakra to come into being and be born. Very simply this is how it may work in practice. I will use the example of writing a book as an illustration:

Step One: Traveling through the Crown Chakra. The affirmation of the Crown Chakra is "The Right to be connected to Spirit". Its purpose is to give us *inspiration*. So in order to write a book, you need to have a good idea!

Step Two: Traveling through the Brow Chakra. The affirmation of the Brow Chakra is "The Right to See and Understand the Truth". It relates to both the third eye (psychic truth) and to cognitive reasoning: In order to write a book, you need to have a vision and a brain!

Step Three: Traveling through the Throat Chakra. The affirmation of the Throat Chakra is "The Right to Hear and Speak the Truth". In other words, in order to write a book a clear authentic voice is needed. Listening is also required as a book is a two-way process: A dynamic between the Author and the Reader.

Step Four: Traveling through the Heart Chakra. The affirmation of the Heart Chakra is "The Right to Give and Receive Love". It's about the breath. In other words, in order to write a book the Author must love the process. The book will be a gift to the world. The act of writing a book is a Sacred Act of Service; that in itself is a gift to the Author.

Step Five: Traveling through the Chakra of the Solar Plexus. The affirmation of the Solar Plexus is "The Right to be Here". In other words, in order to be able to produce a book the Author must be robust and confident enough to feel that their book may have a place in the world and be of value. Ultimately the book must also be robust, confident, deserving to be in the world in its own right and able to stand alone.

Step Six: Traveling through the Sacral Chakra. The affirmation of the Sacral Chakra is "The Right to Give and Receive Pleasure". In other words, the Act of Creation is a sensory tactile experience: a book must be recognized as a thing of Beauty which the Author has enjoyed bringing to the world.

Step Seven: Traveling through the Root Chakra. The affirmation of the Root Chakra is "The Right to Be Here", in other words for a book to be birthed or published it must be original just like every human being; providing insight and uniqueness. Since it has traveled through the body and out into the world it now has a material presence. Ideally it should now give back to the Author, through payment for the book when people buy it, thus completing the cycle by enabling the Author to meet their physical requirements in terms of living on the Earth: core needs such as food, shelter and clothing must be met if not wholly by a book at least partially!

CB continued to show me more. The next image was of a mountain with a Priest sitting on it. Some people were handing the Priest food. Through CB's reaction to this image I saw that this was the old way of doing things. There was no longer to be a separation between the Sacred and the Divine. In our New metaphysical Age the Priest would come down from the mountain and enter the marketplace. The production of the material from a place of respect and holiness means that the marketplace now becomes Sacred. The Priest does not serve the worker and the worker does not serve the Priest in a discon-nected and separated way. There is no longer a divide between the spiritual and the material. We begin to make Heaven on Earth. We start to achieve immanence and become immanent. Or Nirvana; or Bliss. This happens by the Divine manifesting itself in the material world through the actions of each person comprising of the mind, body, spirit and soul of the person; that it manifests through their thoughts, speech and action into the totality of them. In effect, man or woman becomes Divine in the material world!

When writing this section of the book the whole concept of immanence seemed to me to be like a beautiful perfume: I couldn't quite put my finger on it. It felt like a huge energy to be bringing to the light. And where does integration of the masculine and feminine fit into this model? I wasn't the only person intrigued. My editor and friend Leah Kotkes sat up all night considering its implications. She came back with the helpful comments below. I am pleased to include them because she has hit the nail on the head:

What are you really saying is that if the world moved to more acceptance of masculine and feminine within both men and women, and men and women worked to respect and honor and work more as a team, we would invite more grace into the world which would be manifested through the actions of men and women who were more Divine in their thoughts, feelings and actions; that the good will and energy that manifests from good will and peace and acts of tolerance, and acceptance and love and kindness bring into the world and into the heart and soul of man a new energy, and from that energy we could have a better, more peaceful and collaborative and harmonious world? If yes, say this.
– Leah Kotkes, May 2015

You must define your understanding of the word immanence and then continue; it is or it is not the human ability and capacity to live with grace and desire and manifest in your own way a connection and relationship with the Divine outside of self and inside of self; it is the dual journey of discovery of self internally and externally. Not an easy journey; not an easy task but my understanding is that each and every one is drawn to immanence hence the unconscious and conscious 'shift' taking place in our generation; the need for a connection and relationship with the Divine, with a spirituality reality, with something beyond and more important and intrinsic than the material.
– Leah Kotkes, May 2015

What does immanence mean in practice? My understanding is that it means that as we go about our day-to-day life we enter into a state of surrender, grace and appreciation. That we begin to live our life as a prayer. For example when we put a spoonful of honey in our mouths we implicitly understand that in that moment we are consuming a miracle and have awareness and gratitude for every step of the process: from the seed to the pollen, from the pollen to the Bee, from the journey through the sky to the hive, from the winter store of the Bee to the jar and from the jar to the spoon and from the spoon to our mouths. The same goes for when we bake a loaf of bread or pick and eat a blackberry. It means that when we look into the eyes of another human being we truly see them and appreciate them for who they are: for their courage, their grace, their gifts; even for their shadow. That we see the light of the Divine in them; and through our reflection in their eyes we see the Divine in ourselves reflected back.

Chapter Seventeen

Once I had begun to grasp the concept of immanence intellectually, I started to wonder what integrating the masculine and feminine meant in practice. Throughout this book I have talked about how to be a good Angel Channeler. I have to nullify myself or get out of the way. Now I saw that I had an additional task. If as a human I had the potential to make manifest the Divine like CB had said, was it not incumbent upon me to make sure that I was whole and complete in order to do this? I must admit the impetus for this did not come just from myself. Often clients would meet me and say: "I am doing so much work processing and healing myself that I am not being effective in the world!" "What shall I do?" Now if I was answering that question myself I would be quite stern and say (from a lofty and judgmental height): "You must Carry out Tikkun Olam! [Repair of the world!] It's imperative!" But this was not CB's take on things at all. When I tuned in to her she was much gentler; she told me that those people in this generation who are working to change themselves in order to assist in the raising of the Earth's vibration to a new level are engaged in holy and necessary work. That they should be supported and encouraged; praised for their courage. Her comments sent me off on a tangent as they reminded me of the poet Philip Larkin: When I was a student at the University of Hull 35 years ago I often used to see him wandering around the university library. He even smiled at me once or twice. He wrote the poem below:

"This Be The Verse"
By Philip Larkin
They fuck you up, your mum and dad.
They may not mean to, but they do.
They fill you with the faults they had

And add some extra, just for you.

But they were fucked up in their turn
By fools in old-style hats and coats,
Who half the time were soppy-stern
And half at one another's throats.

Man hands on misery to man.
It deepens like a coastal shelf.
Get out as early as you can,
And don't have any kids yourself.
(Philip Larkin, *Collected Poems*, published 1988, Faber and
Faber Ltd. and the Marvell Press; page 180)

Very good clear advice from dear Philip Larkin! While I can take his point and am grateful for the insight, it seems a bit drastic! (But funny!) I think that CB's advice to stop and work to become immanence and have Heaven on Earth is more positive than wiping humans out in one generation!

I reviewed the channeled advice to integrate the masculine and feminine, and put it in the context of my relationships with men. I took notice of CB's insistence that it is incumbent upon each and every one of us to work on ourselves so that we do not hand on 'misery man to man'. I was then prompted to realize I harbored behavior that needed repair in connection to my relationships with men: how I viewed them and how I interacted with them. This isn't going to sound very original but when I pondered this chapter for a long time I had to admit the root of my dysfunction was in my family home. We all go back there don't we, to the beginning to find the answers, and that is where I realized the culture of our home definitely had influenced certain aspects of myself that perhaps had not helped me manage my personal affairs in quite the way I would like to have at home or out in the world.

I can't tell you I like myself in victim-mode, but it was time I saw myself for who I really was and I didn't like that woman very much. I have to admit that, until recently, in some ways I unconsciously carried a profound disrespect and misunderstanding of men, although I loved them in other ways. I was uncomfortable with the unconscious power that I carried as a woman. Let me give a practical example. In 2012, I was in Zack's classroom with a few parents, men and women. We were all cleaning it ready for the new term (that is what happens in Steiner Schools; the parents are responsible for the classroom clean until the kids are old enough to do it themselves). A new parent (a woman) came into the classroom to join us. I took it upon myself to introduce her to the mothers. I said to her, "This is Lucy. This is Sally." When I had finished my two introductions the two fathers got up, held out their hands to her and said: "Hello, I am Peter," and the other said, "Hi, I'm Malcolm." I had failed to introduce the new parent to the fathers in the room!

It honestly had not entered my head to do so; they may as well not have been there. Why had I done this?

My mother's family originated from the East End of London. Like many East End families our family was matriarchal; in our home, the men were never consulted. In fact, it was my grandmother's practice to keep my grandfather in the kitchen. He was a docker. She made it clear to any woman in our midst that would listen to her tale of woe that she had married 'beneath her'. When the 'family' came for tea they were served on china in her front room while my grandfather sat alone in the kitchen. One reason that my grandfather ate alone was that when he was a child during the First World War his classroom was bombed and many children were killed; he sheltered under the falling blackboard and by a lucky accident was saved. This trauma caused my grandfather to have a nervous burping stutter forever after; my grandmother could not tolerate the sound and he was relegated to the kitchen but he never protested. It didn't matter to my grandmother that my grandfather got up at 6am each day to travel to the docks, that he put food on the table; neither did it matter that he could play music by ear, could do *The Times* crossword, speak five languages and was much loved by his comrades in the pub, was a socialist who stood against the Fascist Mosley Blackshirts when they came to march through the East End of London and would not let them pass. My grandmother had decided he was an embarrassment to her, and therefore he had to be invisible when the family visited and he never protested. Hence my lack of respect for men but not my lack of compassion. I loved my grandfather but would never speak my mind about my grandmother's behavior or encourage my grandfather to stand up to her tyranny. But their relationship affected me and it was carried over into my life, in a way I know was not good for me or my perception of men. I had my work cut out for me as I became a young woman in the world. By the time I became a mother and realized my disrespect in the classroom incident I mentioned earlier, I did not like myself very much. There was no excuse for my behavior but I do believe my background was a determining factor. I was born in 1960; my socialization and expectation may be different to yours. I am certainly not supporting my disregard or what today might be regarded as a disrespectful approach towards men or unkindness. I saw that some of my character traits needed repair; that I had work to do. I resolved to change my behavior. I used Radical Forgiveness Therapy to forgive my past, and to integrate it, to come to terms with the fact that I had been exposed to interpersonal relationships which had negatively affected my appreciation and understanding of relationships, respect and communication with men. I also endeavored to realign my feminine energy and intent; the goal to stop me employing distorted denigrating behavior and a lack of good clean communication which was not passive aggressive.

Further, I realized that my response to men was not straightforward either. For example, I was completely shocked at how devoted I was to the man of unrequited love. My love for him expressed itself by wanting to care for him at the deepest level and attend to him because I adored him. This was not a response at the level of equality between the sexes. It was at a level of expressing my femininity in response to his masculinity. In Chapter Fifteen, I referred to our dynamic from the viewpoint of a victim. But this was at one level only; on another level it could be argued that I had my place in the drama. I certainly realized that before I could relate to him decently, respectfully and authentically in actuality he was loving enough to demonstrate extreme patience and kindness at the highest level, while I worked upon removing from my vibration my family's ancestral tendency for the women to control men and treat them as children.

In looking at the whole issue of integration of masculine and feminine I noticed that whenever I had been disrespectful and abusive or angry towards anyone I had diminished myself and lessened my own power and respect for myself. The worst that I had been; the least that I felt that I had any right to be in the world. I had the insight that I behaved at times like a queen bee while I presided over the honey; I certainly had a temper and a sting. When I resorted to using the sting I immobilized myself through self-hatred.

I began to understand what Jung had meant about integrating the shadow. I realized that like a bee I would only sting or react when I felt that my Root Chakra or security was threatened, and usually that was when I felt afraid or upset. I began the work to find out why I was afraid, and I began to realize that in this Divine world providing that I attended to myself and loved myself on a day-to-day level I had no reason to be afraid and no reason to sting. I just had to be disciplined enough to contain myself and disciplined enough to reprogram my reactions. After a lot of honest deep work and a lot of process, I started to feel comfortable in my own skin again: confident and trusting, as though I was living in a state of gratitude and grace. I began to be able to surrender and receive; to feel that I was living my life as a prayer.

Part Three
Extraordinary Life

"Now," he said, "now we're away, now we're clear, we're clean gone, Tenar. Do you feel it?"

She did feel it. A dark hand had let go its lifelong hold upon her heart. But she did not feel joy as she had in the mountains. She put her head down in her arms and cried, and her cheeks were salty and wet. She cried for her years in bondage to a useless evil. She wept in pain because she was free.

What she had begun to learn was the weight of liberty. Freedom is a heavy load, a great and strange burden for the spirit to undertake. It is not easy. It is not a gift given, but a choice made, and the choice may be a hard one. The road goes upwards towards the light; but the laden traveler may never reach the end of it.

"Voyage", page 295, *The Earthsea Quartet* by Ursula Le Guin (Penguin, 1993)

Chapter One

In January 2012, I was on my way to an appointment rushing past the National Gallery in Trafalgar Square in the center of London, one of England's more prominent art galleries, a ten-minute walk from Pall Mall and Buckingham Palace.

Well, on this rainy day at the start of the New Year my Angel CB was pretty verbal:

"Stop, there are Angels in there. Go and look."

To which I replied:

"Sorry, actually no, it's too late. I don't have time. I am late for an appointment." It's not a good idea to deny your Angel; it is tantamount to denying her existence, and CB would not allow me to ignore her. I received further very strong instructions that stopped me in my tracks; it was the Angelic equivalent of being shouted at:

"Go and look NOW."

As I walked into the foyer of the National Gallery I felt there was great excitement around me, coming not only from CB but also from other spiritual guides and my long-dead grandparents. There was a sense of anticipation and celebration as if I were at my twenty-first birthday party and coming of age. But it was CB who was literally doing the prompting. She told me:

"No, not there, go here."

I was propelled forward to the gift shop where in the far corner against the wall were a stack of cut-price yearly calendar-planners with the picture of an Angel on the cover each reduced to 99p.

In retrospect, I should have bought the calendar but I micro-manage and live on a simple rather strict budget so it didn't happen, but I think that CB was telling me something that day: Angels were going to be included in my day-to-day life throughout 2012 and today would be no exception.

But CB was not finished with me yet. I received further messages. I was told to leave the gift shop and enter the gallery rooms upstairs, which I did all the while being directed:

"Go here, go there. No! Up... now left."

Twice I asked:

"Where to now?"

I was directed to a room for the Impressionist paintings. This surprised me because by now I expected CB to take me to the Old Masters. But behind the Van Gogh was a picture of a 16th century Seer: *The Cumaean Sibyl with Putto*, 1651, by Guercino.

A Putto or winged cherub representing the omnipresence of God hovered behind the Seer in the background and I was told by CB:

"There you are. This is you."

I stood in front of this painting for a very long time. I was utterly transported. I am afraid to say that I forgot about my appointment. I found the whole encounter with the 16th Century Seer and Putto awe-inspiring.

When I finally got home I looked up the meaning of the word 'seer'. The Oxford paperback *Dictionary & Thesaurus*[1] said Seer means: "clairvoyant, fortuneteller, oracle, prophet, prophetess, psychic, Sybil, soothsayer, vaticinator". I read: "A Seer is one who sees with spiritual eyes. S(He) perceives the meaning of that which seems obscure to others; therefore (s)he is an interpreter and clarifier of eternal truth. (S)He foresees the future from the past and the present."

At that time, I was startled. I didn't see myself in that role of a Seer supported by a Putto representing the omnipresence of God. I draw back from making prophecies. I find it rewarding to work with clients who are seeking to determine their own path through their own inner knowledge. I certainly have no intention of taking on the responsibility of telling people the future, and perhaps getting it wrong, self-doubt being my issue. Yet, here I was the day after being propelled through the gallery rooms of the National Gallery by my own personal Angel who I call CB because she had something of importance to tell me: that I am a Seer; that perhaps I possess powers or abilities to enable people to see things more clearly, especially helping them perhaps access the Divine for the good of their lives and to help others.

I mulled over this idea for a minute and then found myself laughing. The whole idea was preposterous. I was an ordinary person with an 'intuition' like most people, I assumed. Jewish Scripture teaches that women are born with a *bina yisera*, which translates from Hebrew to English to mean an inner wisdom. Perhaps this is what CB was trying to tell me, that I should utilize my innate God-given wisdom to help more people.

Later, I wrote in my Blog telling the story of my encounter with a 'Seer' in the National Gallery. While I was writing, a new thought surfaced almost organically: if I am to help others with my innate wisdom surely I should be helping myself first. Perhaps CB was showing me that I needed to look after myself better. When I next tuned in to CB I asked her which diet I should follow. Her 'holy' reply was quick in coming:

- Eat food with least suffering contained within it.
- Be without meat, cow's milk and bread.
- You do not need sugar to make your life sweet and for you seaweed is good.
- As you raise your vibration you will need less food, but also you need to run and dance in the world.
- Rise from your stupor and be active.

Why was CB advising me to diet and to take on such specific eating and lifestyle habits? Perhaps she had shown me the Sibyl who was overweight to prompt me to look after myself physically. Now writing this I am ashamed. I realize that I had allowed myself to be defined by my body and had used my body size as a reason to denigrate and put myself down. A poor show for an

Angel Reader who prides herself in seeing the light of the Divine in everyone and encouraging them to live at their full potential.

As I was not then disciplined enough to diet or increase my activity schedule, my new diet did not last more than a week following CB's advice. But I see now that she did not direct me to a painting in the National Gallery to induce me to write a Blog or to undertake a diet. My personal Angel Celestial Bell was telling me I had a gift and it was time to use it more wisely; she was telling me now is the time and however long I ignore or disregard her message it will make no difference. This was my 'calling'. I had a job to do; it was about time I started serving the universe with a gift that has its source in the universe. CB was telling me that she is a conduit for the messages I am destined to hear; I must take my responsibility seriously.

The Angelic intervention I received in January 2012 was presenting the truth and preparing me for my future.

In March 2013, I began to work as an Angel Channeler in Watkins Books, Cecil Court, London WC2. Watkins Books is the oldest esoteric bookshop in the United Kingdom. I work from a small booth with a red velvet tablecloth giving channeled Angel Readings given to me by CB, as well as energy healing and intuitive coaching. Today, I am in fact a modern-day 'Seer'. However, I still rarely practice divination or tell fortunes. Even if I do clearly see the future for that person I hardly ever disclose it. My task is more important. With CB's help I am lucky enough to be able to see the potential in people and to be able to reflect back to them the gifts that they are bringing to the world. This in turn helps them to appreciate themselves and to be able to take their place in the world. To shine more brightly if they want to and to partake in the repair of the world; if they want to.

Watkins Books is about a stone's throw from the National Gallery. This position came to me a little over a year after the National Gallery experience. In March, CB told me that Watkins Books had need of me so I went to London and visited unprompted into the store.

The Watkins staff knew me because I had supplied them previously with Angel CDs and scented candles, and had given staff informally channeled Angel Readings. I walked in and explained that CB had told me to come, and asked them what help they needed. Luckily, because Watkins is an esoteric bookshop, no one found this announcement strange. They did indeed have need of me because their in-house Palmist was about to take a Sabbatical. So I worked several days a week in his place and was retained on a part-time basis once he returned. The position at Watkins Books led to my articles being published in *Kindred Spirit Magazine*[2] and to the encouragement and impetus for this book.

I have a new policy now. I listen to CB. I write down what she says and I think about it and then work out how to use the information to the advantage of my work as an Angel Channeler, Energy Healer and Intuitive Coach. I now eat far less processed foods, meat and poultry, choosing instead to eat organic food and fish whenever possible.

A friend of mine, who is interested in nutrition, is supporting me to change my diet and eat more healthy foods. I also took on more exercise. Even if many Seers portrayed in art carry weight I know now I do not want to have my life on Earth restricted because I find it difficult to move around due to unhealthy diet and exercise choices. But that is a different reason for wanting to lose weight than just wanting to fit in with the images of beauty decided by convention.

Chapter Two

My extraordinary life really began when I consciously connected with my personal Angel Celestial Bell aka CB: when I listened to her most attentively the day I visited the National Gallery in London and was shown the painting of the Seer as I described in the previous chapter of this book.

Today, three years on, when I want to talk to my personal Angel, to ask for help or guidance or advice for myself or for my clients, all I do is sit quietly and connect with her; talk to her out loud or in my head. The professional work I do today relies on this connection, this relationship, this place of trust and respect between us.

It has taken me five years to get to this union with Celestial Bell. In the beginning I resisted Angelic messages and images; I was too overwhelmed. As time passed I came to terms with my psychic attributes and abilities. Then I trained, and I still study and train, to improve and develop my skills. Today, I am not the person I was in the beginning of my conscious awareness of mysticism and all these beyond normal in my life. I have gained experience and training but equally so I have taken the time and made a conscious effort to do an inventory of my character traits and my personal and familial history, and I have worked on myself. My goal was to become a better person, a more informed and equipped human being; a stronger and more effective physical, emotional and spiritual conduit. I have invested hours of time challenging and improving my mind; my intellect is sharper. Life still has its challenges but I am more ready to deal with them from the treasure chest of my life experience and practical skills.

My journey can be your journey in your way. You too have a personal Angel; we all do!

This section of the book is not designed to offer evidence of major miracles I have experienced or witnessed since I began my professional work in the field of the spiritual. It is a practical section of the book; to demonstrate to you how I grounded myself in the material, in the physical, to be able to manage and contain the spiritual work that I do. It offers pragmatic insight into the day-to-day life of a Spiritualist.

In the beginning when I realized I had special gifts, I used them to manifest what I wanted materially. I started out my career as a Consultant and Fundraiser. I was an effective professional; on one project I was able to raise more than £1.5 million for the London Borough of Hillingdon; I do not recall this taking me too much effort. It seemed to me at the time whenever I was presented with a financial target I could 'conjure up' what I needed as well as manifest all my needs. Once, I could not find my tape measure: I walked out of the door of my house and a perfectly good tape measure lay on the pavement! Other times, when I needed contract work I attracted large contracts with ease; going through appropriate and ethical process I must add! I had a good reputation; I did not advertise my consultancy services. I was often approached and offered work or found one contract led to another with an associate I met in the current project. Before I came to know my personal Angel I was aware of my psychic abilities and in my own way used them to my advantage. This afforded me a certain level of self-assurance; I was confident that I could always attract what I needed in the form of money whenever I needed to.

This 'fairy tale' reality in relation to my fiscal income changed in 2010. With a new government in England a new dawn arrived; a new approach to the funding of local government and the public sector contracted; a 10% contraction in the public sector translated itself into a 99% contraction in contracts to be awarded to consultants. I was totally unprepared for this. The socioeconomic and political milieu in which I operated brought with it a shift in my ability to manifest abundance. Although my client contacts wanted me to continue to work for them, they now were in crisis, occupied in fighting for their own livelihoods and trying to protect the services that they had provided; dealing with the impact of the most savage cuts. My work had concerned expansion. The new landscape was about contraction and there was nothing that we could do about it. We all entered a new climate of instability and great change as well as loss and grief. We watched in disbelief as our skilled and beautiful work was systematically dismantled. This change in circumstance brought with it a change in my attitude to how I embraced my spirituality.

By necessity I moved away from a focus on what I had in the material world and began to appreciate what I had in my personal life and aspects of my life that we cannot measure: family, friendships, relationships, health, happiness to name but a few.

It is possible that if I would have asked for a manifestation of wealth and abundance at this time I would have received it. Many of my consultant contemporaries moved into well-paying jobs, or found a niche and survived somehow. But for some reason I felt very affected in an empathic way to the shift in energy and feeling amongst my fellow work colleagues. I also realized that I no longer wanted to be part of a sphere of being that was about fixing the world from a perspective of 'us' and 'them', swanning in as the powerful professional and then exiting. I wanted to be part of things, part of a community; even if this meant that there would be less money.

I consciously decided to opt out of the material sphere of life. I wanted to embark on a spiritual quest for enlightenment and self-actualization. It was a risk but I felt it was one worth taking; the timing seemed right. Although I can rationalize it in this way, in truth there was not really an option. Every promise that was offered for consultancy came to a dead end; while every opportunity to work in the spiritual realm seemed to shine as an enormous light and bear fruit in remarkable ways. Hence this book!

I am writing these words with care. I like to be abundant; I enjoyed earning well and living well early in my career. I would have been happy if life had not changed and I had not taken a new pathway but the times changed, which in turn changed me and helped me realize I wanted something more in an ironically less abundant time of change. This period in my life involved an interim period where I experienced a transition of thought, speech and action. When I began to build a new bridge to a new life and a new way of thinking. It was also a time of not very much money; of living simply; of living without the comforts I had enjoyed for so many years. The transition was not simple; in fact it was challenging, frustrating and many times I felt uncomfortable, I was frightened and I felt immense strain and concern for my emotional well-being and the future security of my family.

Looking back on this time period of five years I truly appreciate the decisions I made even though I had no idea where the choices would take me. Today, I am richer for the experiences I endured and the challenges I overcame. My family and I learned to live on a wing and a prayer for much of this time but the times are changing.

Many of the stories that follow are stories of the personal miracles that occurred in this time and there are also stories I wanted to share because my hope is that they will help you to be able to heal any wounds that you may be carrying, or help you to set out on your own journey.

Sometimes we have no choice: we have to change, we are forced to change, change is imposed on us. When this time comes we have in principle two choices: to rise up to the challenge or let ourselves fall lower and lower into despair. I chose the high road. But this did not mean that in times I was not in despair.

I hope this section of my book encourages you to remember you are never alone, and help is within reach inside of you and all around you. Open your eyes, open your heart, open your soul and ask for what you need and be ready to receive.

Chapter Three

Life for me has definitely improved; I thank my personal Angel;
I thank all the people I trained with that I mentioned in Part Two;
I thank each and every client, they have been my greatest
teachers. Life was not also so rosy and happy for me. There was
a time when I was living in a family home where there was no
order, no money to account for; there was a lot of suffering and
sadness. When I was twelve, my parents finally divorced. As I
recounted in Part One of this book, we were not a prosperous
family and 'drama' and 'pain' were frequent visitors in our
home. I have explained how as a child I was supported greatly
by both my grandmothers, by my grandfather and my six aunts
and uncles so I was not without love. Although my mother is
loving to the point of self-sacrifice, there was an emotional gap.
There was a lack of a father; my father was rarely present in our
home, and when he was there was often mayhem. My
relationship with my father broke down altogether after my
parents divorced. By the time I was sixteen, I lost touch with my
father completely.

Once I reached fifty, I worried about my lack of contact with
my father. I was afraid of hearing that he had died, and what
would I then do? Would I attend the funeral of a father that I no
longer knew and had not been reconciled with? It seemed too
painful and complicated. I spoke with my personal Angel about
this situation and waited for her reply. But nothing came through
that route. There was just silence.

Then one day 192.com, a UK-based telecommunications
company, sent an e-mail flyer asking whether I wanted to receive
a postcard from the past? Inviting me to find someone who was
missing in my life. On the spur of the moment I entered my
father's details, the area where I had heard that he was living and
his date of birth. To my amazement back came his address and

telephone number. So I wrote to him asking if he wanted to be in touch. After all, I pointed out, he wasn't getting any younger and at some point it would be too late.

I did not receive a reply to my letter. Time went on. I thought, perhaps he hadn't received my letter. After all, I couldn't understand why he did not reply to me. When I thought about my own two sons, and the fact I would not imagine being without them in my life, I felt a great rush of compassion and love for my father. I had this great need to see him again; to find a way to forgive the past that I related to him and begin again this time on new terms with him. Time went on. Another flyer arrived from 192.com, and spurred on by this I called his number. The phone was answered by the woman whom he had left our family for and she passed me to my father.

My father and I spoke on the telephone for twenty minutes. Sadly, my father told me that he didn't wish to be in contact with me, even by phone. He said he had received my letter but decided not to reply as there was too much water under the bridge, and he was too long in the tooth, plus whenever he thought of me he saw me as my mother. I think he felt so guilty he could not speak to me without considering what he had done to her and to my brothers and me.

Although it is impossible here to convey the degree of pain his reaction brought me I am proud of how I conducted myself. I explained to him that although I am my mother's daughter, I am also his daughter, and while he may not wish to be in contact with me, I would be pleased to hear from him. And also that within my community in Totnes I was much loved.

After this conversation, I went to bed for three days. I couldn't speak to anyone or see anyone. I was so stunned by his reaction and in too much pain to talk. In the end, I texted a dear friend; I shared what had happened. He was in London but took the trouble to support me. He was most loving. I was unable to recount out loud what had happened between my father and me;

it took him three days to verbally extract the story from me, which he did with his customary skill, care and kindness. Once I could speak about the incident, I felt myself healing. When I was ready I asked for my personal Angel's help. Celestial Bell comforted me through a dream. In the dream, I saw my father's brother Vic who had been a surrogate father to me while I was growing up. Uncle Vic was standing in his garden. I ran to him as I always had. He said: "Hello, our Wendy." I felt the full force of his love that he had always given me. Although not my birth father, I had been treasured and loved by Uncle Vic every day. There had never been a birthday or Christmas missed by Uncle Vic; I had always been provided for. He had been a staunch guardian and the insight that I was given in the dream was that, until he died, Uncle Vic had been as a father to me and that he continues to watch over me and love me. So in reality there was no gap where a father should be except the one left by Uncle Vic who died when he was only sixty-seven years old, when I was 43 years old, which was 12 years ago. Even though I have missed him dreadfully ever since, the morning after my dream I realized he was still with me, and always had been!

What I learned from this situation with my father and the subsequent dream is this. Because my biological father didn't want me in his life, that doesn't mean that everyone in the world doesn't want me. What was happening between my father and me had nothing to do with me; it was all about my father and his lack of capacity to give and to be kind. My personal Angel CB instructed me to take the following outlook: "Stand in your own shoes and have compassion for all that your father has lost. Know that you are treasured and loved."

The reason I share this story with you is simple. We begin our lives in the homes of parents who try their best sometimes under very challenging circumstances; but we, as children, do not know all the facts and nor should we. All we know is what we feel and see and hear; and we do not hear everything, but what we do feel and see forms what we are and how we feel and think about ourselves.

The spiritual journey I have taken since I accepted the responsibility for my psychic abilities and forged a good working relationship with my personal Angel CB has prompted me to undertake a lot of spiritual training. This training has not only equipped me to help others and guide them, it has helped strengthen my spiritual resolve and my spiritual makeup. I was only able to phone my father with the view of reestablishing some sort of relationship with him because I was more equipped to deal with him and my past, and because I had the support and guidance of CB.

There is a postscript to this story about my father, which looked like ending in pain and loss.

While still engaged in writing this book, on my fifty-third birthday in 2013, out of the blue I received a birthday card from my father, with words in gold gilt "To my daughter" and addressed to "Wendy Jane", his pet name for me. A month or so later I sent another card back for his birthday and then suddenly received a telephone call. He would be in Devon; please may he visit? He came with his wife and spent an afternoon with my family and myself. It was truly a special day for all of us. My father and I went for a walk alone and heard each other out. He had heard of my divorce via my mother, via my eldest brother, and said that he wanted to check out that I was OK. It was immeasurably healing and I have deep gratitude for this opportunity, which was momentous to me.

If I hadn't been carrying out so much work and process to remove projections and be able to come from a place of love and compassion, not need and pain, I would not ever have been able to receive him. As I am writing this I also cannot say that we went back into any full relationship. I telephoned him once and spoke with him and he has not called back – yet. Perhaps he saw that despite everything I was strong and managing – I don't know.

What I do know is through that one meeting I am at peace in relation to him. Thank goodness for my spiritual training and CB's support. Thank goodness to 192.com! I have gratitude to my father too, for ultimately having enough courage to turn around and face his past.

Chapter Four

On Valentine's Day – February 14, 2013 – you may or may not know there was a worldwide campaign against Domestic Violence.[3] I wasn't involved in the organizing and am not sure what went on elsewhere in the world but in Totnes, Devon, England, there was a silent march from the bottom of town and up the high street, followed by dancing in the Civic Square and an evening Cabaret. This was to fundraise for educational and healing initiatives against Domestic Violence, as well as contributing to the worldwide message that violence towards women is not acceptable.

There had been a lot of preparation beforehand with many people attending lessons to learn a special dance for the day and an art workshop held to decorate the Civic Hall. For me, taking part in this event was an enormous privilege and healed many wounds. By now you may have realized that I grew up in a house with a father who suffered from outbursts of anger, and know firsthand how hard it is to both live with and recover from domestic violence. I have carried out a great deal of work on myself to enable me to function 'normally' in the company of people that trigger emotions related to past experiences. So I found myself standing in Totnes Civic Square in tears amongst the love and the singing and dancing and a great outpouring of heart energy. There was so much generosity, good sense and also authentic and genuine support from both men and women, not only for ourselves in the square but for sisters and brothers around the world.

I phoned my mother during the dancing and left a record of the singing on her answer phone; I knew that she would be thrilled to hear it. Speaking with her later, to thank her for her courage and for protecting me the best that she could and giving me all that she could, she said: "Well even now your father denies it." Later this comment made me think of how it's not only violence that can be denied but that Spirituality can also be denied. For example, I learnt to be circumspect in relation to whom I tell that I am an Angel Channeler and Healer, and I tend to keep quiet about being fairly psychic.

I don't know about you but I have also had a great deal of difficulty integrating spirituality, healing and Angels into my 'day job'; in fact I didn't manage to integrate it. It was incompatible. I had to give up the day job.

The Valentine's Day campaign that took place in Totnes turned into a empowering day for many of us including me; I was granted more clarity about my past experience with family domestic violence and felt healed and encouraged by all the kindness and support on offer through the day into the night. I especially loved that some men had taken the trouble to learn the Valentine's Day dance and had shown up in support.

When I asked my personal Angel what she was feeling, CB said:

Every human has the right to live in peace and dignity. Imagine if all the mothers and all the women in the world were empowered and said, "No," all violence would cease in all instances to all beings (including animals). Humans are beginning to raise their consciousness through care with process, and through acknowledging the Divine mother. Know that everyone involved in violence and abuse are victims. Exercise compassion and forgiveness – affirm your sisters. Love and appreciate them. Love and appreciate yourself. Be assured of the shift. The more faith that you have, the more the shift will be held.

As usual Spirit had the last word. I came away from the dancing that day to walk Lily our dog who was furious at my neglect to find a rainbow stretching across the sky above my house. It was a sign of Heaven meeting Earth. I felt truly blessed to be alive and to be part of 'The Great Shift'.

There is more to add to this story. In the spring of this year 2015, *Kindred Spirit* asked me to attend a weekend workshop called Awakening of Love or AOL.[4] This took place in Pax Lodge, Belsize Park, London. My job was to attend and take part in the course and write a review. I did this. But the course impacted on me in more ways than I included in the review so I will tell you about it here.

Going into Pax Lodge, the venue, my heart was touched unexpectedly. Pax Lodge is the headquarters of the Girl Guide Movement. I had always felt a little bit ambivalent towards the Scouting and Girl Guide movement, judging it as over controlling. But standing in Pax Lodge I understood how embracing the Girl Guide and Scouting movements have been; how egalitarian; how they worked for the good. This is why: I have already explained how the home that I came from could be chaotic. In Pax Lodge I realized that the Girl Guide Movement and Scouting had brought the gift of order to many chaotic homes through teaching and acknowledging a wide range of skills to young people who might not otherwise have had access to them. That they were responsible for instilling order and showing a different way of being that must have helped young people to climb out of chaos regardless of their background. That it was indeed *possible* to climb out of chaos; that ultimately it doesn't matter where we come from, it's where we arrive that counts.

Then I received an unexpected validation in the dining room. Aged 55 and after all the work that I had done on myself, this hit the spot. The healing came from a couple of chalk posters made by guides. They gave a message that six out of ten women experience violence in their lifetime. Although I was sad, angry at the implications of this, it also felt as if a weight dropped from my shoulders. I suddenly realized that I wasn't alone. I wasn't part of the minority; I was part of the majority. I had not ever been that open about the fact that our family had domestic violence in it. I was ashamed and worried that owning this personal history would cause people to project upon me that I was not whole; that I carried wounds that may impact on my judgment and have people see me as a poor thing, as a victim. I had too much pride for that. I walked out of the dining room in Pax Lodge a different woman to the one that walked in. In that moment I had accepted my past and realized that it did not define me.

I also came away from the AOL course a different person. Now I need to be careful here because I am bound by confidentiality; but I don't think that it will be doing anyone any harm if I tell you that at times in the course there were participants achieving personal insights that brought them to tears. The number of men crying struck me. It was so healing for me to see men being able to cry and admit their vulnerability, work on themselves, be prepared to change; previously I had thought this to be the preserve of women only. Not So! How wonderful it is to be born in our times and to be able to participate in 'The Great Shift': the integration of the masculine and feminine; of the Spiritual and the Material and also talk to Angels!

Chapter Five

In the summer of 2012, I was living with my two adult sons in Devon. We lived on a simple budget; the boys were at Steiner School and university respectively. I was beginning on a regular basis to uphold my emerging work as an Angel Channeler and Energy Healer. CB is never far away; when I asked her for help it was always given. But even though clients came into my life things were quite challenging economically in these early days of reestablishing myself.

One day we faced the prospect of not having any money at all as no one had booked in for a healing session, and for the first time in my adult life I was concerned that we would not have money for food. In the morning, I asked CB to help me, but during the day no help arrived.

At nine o'clock that night there was a knock on the door. A friend was standing there with a stranger. She asked me if I could offer her friend Bed and Breakfast (B&B) as he had nowhere to stay overnight; the guest offered to pay £30.00. Of course, I would offer B&B if it meant the difference between eating and not eating. I agreed and the guest said he had to go to bring his suitcase. But no one returned. At midnight, my friend came to my house to say the guest had fallen asleep on her coach and she felt that it would be mean to wake him up! She felt it only proper to bring me the £30.00 as it had been agreed I would offer my home for B&B. Initially I refused the payment but she insisted I take it. So I did. Once upon a time, I wouldn't have accepted it as I used to earn a very nice salary in my government job. But at that time I was establishing myself in a new profession and was relying on the miracle of a good word spreading about my skills and attributes as a psychic. I was very thankful, and although it was given in the form of human assistance I am convinced that I had received help through Angelic intervention.

Chapter Six

One day in November 2013, I consciously asked my personal Angel Celestial Bell if I could have some presents! I was struggling a bit just getting along with the day-to-day life. I was still looking to the material to define me and I was fed up with managing on just a wing and a prayer. Everything felt so heavy and lonely: looking back on this day now I cringe a bit because I think that I was being self-indulgent, asking CB if I could have some gifts! But never mind – that was then and now is now.

This is what happened: I had made up a running list of all my difficulties. The liturgy of discontent went as follows:

a) Although we were living in a good house, we were now living outside of our beloved Totnes and I found it too quiet and far from everything and everyone I knew.

b) I felt under pressure with this book, which was sitting (on the laptop) waiting for me to finish it. In my circle, everyone else was also waiting for me to finish it (editor, friends, and future readers, CB, family).

c) On the table a store catalogue glinting with festive gifts was beckoning me.

There was I, safely cocooned in procrastination, exhausted and lonely. I like people and can dislike discipline. CB was continually telling me: "You must finish the book." In desperation, I asked my Angel: "Please could I have something nice happen today to help me finish the book; to motivate me out of my inertia into action – please..."

Gifts began to arrive over the next three days. This is what happened:

On the first day, a book arrived unexpectedly through the post as a gift from a friend: *Initiation* by Elisabeth Haich which kept me so engrossed all loneliness dispersed – as well as giving me some instruction that I needed. This instruction related to operating in the spiritual realm, rather than the material, and also gave a detailed example of Past Life Regression: most insightful and useful.

The second day of asking when I thought I couldn't cope with the endless hours of solitary work, while out shopping for milk, I met a friend who is a traveler, explorer and a wise Shaman. We skipped off to nearby Dartmoor to look for edible mushrooms; we met with no success but instead were treated to rainbows and rural beauty in all its splendor after a downpour which left sparkling dewdrops in our midst.

On the third day of asking, I went to the bank to see about setting myself up properly in business again. As mentioned earlier, my consultancy business had dissolved. At that time I was still liable to sink into fear however much I told myself, "Look ahead to where you are going. Do not look from where you came." The meeting with the business advisor was helpful; I was encouraged to realize that all was not lost and that I could be in business again.

The fourth day was the best because I was directed by CB to go up on to the Moors; I wasn't quite sure why but I was told: "Go this way. Go to Badgers Holt, there is a gift for you."

So there I was going up steep hills thinking, why? What? But listening to my inner voice and inner intuition nonetheless, and following it.

I didn't have to travel as far as Badgers Holt because on the way I found my gift, a series of beautiful rainbows one of which shone across the morning moon; it was 9am. This I have never seen before and couldn't capture it on my camera, perhaps because it was so very sacred, but I have it etched in my memory.

Sitting beneath the rainbow all care dropped away and I could laugh at myself for my impatience and lack of self-compassion. Best of all a friend living in London had been ill with high blood pressure and refusing medication. This had caused me days and nights of endless worry. Before my jaunt on the Moors I had received a phone call telling me he had accepted medication. Sitting under the rainbow that day I felt extreme gratitude for this turn of events as his illness had sent him inward. I had missed him being present for me, as his care and love enhances my life. You can see that not only did I want him better for his own sake but also for my sake!

In the Jewish faith rainbows are seen as special because they link Heaven to Earth and because they symbolize hope. After the flood, God promised Noah that He would never again bring a flood that would destroy the world. A rainbow is a reminder of this covenant that God made with Noah, his descendants, and all living creatures. Therefore, upon seeing a rainbow in the sky, we recite the following blessing:

Blessed are You, Lord our God, King of the universe, who remembers the covenant, and is faithful to His covenant, and keeps His promise.

Even if you do not wish to use this blessing because it is not right for you, then perhaps if you see a rainbow you may wish to give your own expression of thanks.

The rainbow gave me hope and strength to go on, and I was soon back writing minus procrastination and with my heart full of abundance. It was a fantastic gift, consolidated by CB's message, which was: "The dwelling of eyes upon a rainbow raises the body's vibration to one of inner Joy. Rainbows are freely available to everyone – the eyes just have to be open enough to see them!"

Chapter Seven

This story concerns a second intervention from the Archangel Raphael. Have you ever read the story of the man who was looking for God? He searched the world for God, and finally he reached a hut. He was told: "God is in that hut, you may see Him if you look inside." The man stood outside and considered for a long time. In the end he didn't go in. He just shook his head and went away again without looking.

I had been behaving a bit like that man. Focusing on the journey and afraid to arrive. In January 2014, I was given implicit guidance by my personal Angel Celestial Bell to move to London and to go and work in South End Green, in Hampstead in North London. I was told exactly where to go and which place to work. At this time while my financial resources were meager, many of my family and friends had supported me every step of the way with my training and the launch of my new career in the spiritual realm. I knew I had to find more work and this move was inevitable. CB's guidance was insistent and specific. Although I was terrified I followed it, condensing down our family's household possessions until they could be contained and stored in a friend's basement. My son Zachary had asked if he could spend some time living with his father; this request came at a good time. I agreed; I felt it was a good opportunity for him. The proviso was that it was to be a temporary arrangement. I told him my plan; I intended to put our belongings into storage and move to London and commute back to Devon to see him until I knew the next stage of the journey I had to take. My goal was to live back in Devon with him, but first I had to go on a new adventure; he understood.

When I arrived in London in April 2014 my former mother-in-law Helen took me into her home in an almost Biblical fashion and was exceptionally kind and supportive of my plan to make a go of it in London as a mystic. I spent some time looking up my old contacts and skirting around South End Green. I was deeply afraid of looking for work, or even asking. After so much change and upheaval how would it be if I had got everything wrong and been mistaken? Perhaps I was just on my own wild goose chase. The situation was made worse because I was given, through CB's guidance, a specific place to go in South End Green, Hampstead. And in my mind I was not going to be received in that place. I spent a few weeks almost playing rather than going here: I went to Cambridge with a friend; I spent a few days writing a report in my friend's house in Suffolk. I went back to Devon for a few days to see my sons Josh and Zachary. Basically, I went about my business except looking to work in South End Green.

Finally, I plucked up courage and went into the place that I had been directed to. It is called The House of Mistry. I started by asking for an appointment; I wanted to ask the shop to stock the candles that I promote. I went into the shop to be told by the pharmacist that there was no need for an appointment; the owner would look at the candles now. I went to the car and collected the candles and went back to the shop only to be met by a reception committee of women waiting to see Dr. Mistry, the renowned Ayurvedic Doctor who practices from there.

As I unpacked the candles the women crowded around me and bought all of them. Not only that, they seemed to recognize me as a Healer and there was that lovely flash of luminosity that comes when the Earth seems to split open and the Divine seems to be present. And one of the women, by coincidence or synchronicity another red-headed Jewish woman, and like me a Healer, immediately mentioned Angels, telling me that they were to be found within Jewish teachings and spoke to me of the story of Tobias and Raphael, which is given in the Dead Sea Scrolls. It was an unlikely place to be given a biblical message: a chemist's in South End Green. I thought it might be a message from an Angel coming through a human so I looked it up when

I got home. These days it's easy to look on the Internet. A simple search via Google soon had my curiosity satisfied. When I read the story I felt that my instinct was right; I was being given a message of hope. In the story, the Angel Raphael walks alongside Tobias on a journey in disguise. He is his friend and companion. A dog accompanies them. The purpose of the journey is fourfold. It is to find a means of healing Tobias' father who was made blind due to an act of kindness. He had helped to bury someone. In the Jewish faith this meant that he was unclean until certain rites were performed. Because he was technically unclean, rather than going home that night he had slept outside, where he became blind because sparrows pooped in his eyes. Now it was imperative for Tobias to undertake the journey to a far away town to collect a debt owed to his father and regain his family's lost wealth. We hear how Tobias also had the task of casting out a demon that was possessing a woman who was to be his future wife. We can see in the tale that the Archangel Raphael offers Tobias advice and assistance in the dangerous journey, but that Tobias had to listen to him and take action himself. While he was being assisted, he was not being passively saved or rescued.

I liked reading this as I think that it is important to understand that Angels do not want to help us at the expense of us becoming dependent on them; we are the ones who must make our way in the world so that we can learn and grow. Sometimes we need to take risks and action to uphold the values that we hold dear to us, and protect and look after our families. The story of Tobias and Raphael showed the courage of Tobias and the gentle and practical support of the Archangel Raphael who was on hand to help Tobias in the casting out of a demon.

I was glad that this story had been brought to my attention. It helped give me courage and it also gave me guidance. In the story of Tobias, I saw that sometimes the most loving, compassionate action is to walk in companionship and silence alongside a friend, and assist them. And not to rush in and act on their behalf to fix everything.

Tobias left his family to undertake a journey. I did the same. It comforted me to hear that Tobias achieved his aims of recovering his family's wealth and the means to heal his father's blindness. He also found his wife on this journey, although he had to fight a battle with demons for her.

All of the deeper messages I read into Tobias' story gave me strength for my own life journey. I needed to have faith, believe my journey had purpose; I felt the intervention by Archangel Raphael as most positive and was immeasurably comforted.

As I had sold all the candles that day in The House of Mistry, I suggested to the store manager they stock them and I would promote them. This has since materialized. Not only that, but this eventually led to me being able to offer a clinic from there. I worked from The House of Mistry as an Angel Channeler, Energy Worker and Intuitive Coach every other Monday. CB had sent me to the right address.

Later that day CB consolidated her message; I was urged by her to go to Hampstead Heath. I wondered why but couldn't glean an answer. I went back to Hampstead and although tired because it was late I climbed to a favorite spot on the Heath and along came a flock of green parakeets, swooping and tumbling about over my head. Joyously having a lot of fun I think. I always have to look twice at these birds, as they are so unexpected in our English landscape that I think that I am imagining them. A bit like my reaction and relationship to Angels! Angels and parakeets teach me to trust in and believe my perception. The next day I was given the following Angel reading:

"Be assured that you are not journeying alone. There is support for each step. Do not doubt your vision or your judgment. Do not forget to exercise gratitude for your journey. All is well and all will be well."

Chapter Eight

In December 2014, I was standing in a Jewish bakery in Edgware and the woman next to me bought one mince pie. It struck me as funny, so I laughed.

"Why are you laughing at me?" she said.

"I am not laughing 'At You'! Laughing 'With You'! Because it seems incongruous to be buying a mince pie in a Jewish bakery especially at this time of year."

It was the week of the Jewish Festival of Chanukah – and about to be the Christian festive holidays too.

"But mince pies taste good," she said. "Even though I do agree with you, it does seem incongruous doesn't it?"

We both laughed.

Outside the store, I then asked her if she lived locally as I was new in Edgware. She said yes; she had recently moved into the area about eighteen months ago, returning to London from overseas only a few years before. I asked her what her name was. She said: "I am Leah Kotkes."

"What do you do?" I said.

She told me she was a writer, and book and magazine editor, and she mentors writers.

Just like that I found myself an editor for this book, and a writing coach. One of Leah's strengths is editorial strategic inter-vention; in our first meeting within a week, she formulated a new strategy for this book. Before my eyes it became clear how this book would be structured and she made it very clear what she felt I needed to do to create a coherent, compelling, informative story for the intelligent and inquisitive reader.

We began our work together straightaway with a schedule in place for weekly editorial status meetings. I was on my way. If I had timed my visit to the bakery five minutes either way I would have missed meeting Leah Kotkes altogether; she rarely goes out and about shopping so focused is she on her current schedule of writing and studying. But that day she had popped out for five minutes to get a little something in the spirit of Chanukah to have with a cup of tea and so we met. And we have met over many cups of tea since but without the mince pies; we are both now are trying to break the habit of sugar and flour! Long may this last – as well as our new friendship; for I have truly found a loyal, supportive friend in my editor and writing coach.

And if that synchronicity is not a sprinkling of Angel Dust – and mince pie – I don't know what is!

Chapter Nine

This is a strange, whimsical story and a story in two parts of events that truly happened to me. It does not concern the realm of Angels; it concerns the realm of nature spirits.

In the late spring of 2013 my Shaman friend, the one that I mentioned earlier in Part Three, Chapter Six, who is a private person who wouldn't like me to give her name, invited me on a Wild Food Walk. She likes to walk with people and teach them about being able to safely eat food from the wild because she believes, as I do, that it is everyone's right to be well fed and have access to good wholesome food. But choosing to eat from the wild requires some skill, as it can be easy to confuse foods and be poisoned. You need to know what you are doing, especially if mushrooms are involved; but there are other plants that can be equally dangerous.

On this day in the late spring when there were some edible violets to be found, abundant masses of wild garlic to be picked for pesto sauce, my Shaman friend took me to a stream that ran from the River Dart over the Moors and into Totnes. She pointed out a tall feathery plant growing in the wet streamside mud and told me that its name was Hemlock Water Dropwort; one of the most poisonous plants on Earth.

My Shaman friend then went on to recount that at the beginning of the 20th century six young men had brought their cows down from the Moors for the day and grazed them near this very spot. Hemlock Water Dropwort can be confused with parsley, or hawthorn leaves or even the top of celery. These young men thought that the plant was the benign herb, parsley, and added the leaves to their sandwiches. They all fell asleep on the bank of the River; only one of the six woke up that day.

I looked at the Hemlock Water Dropwort and shivered at its power. Then I tuned in to the energy of this plant. Looking at it through my third eye, I felt it to be fey and fairylike, a woman's plant; a tool that may most likely be used by women. Forgive me for recounting this: it's what came to my mind. Within its energy I saw elemental spirits; danger and enchantment. I was glad to leave the Hemlock Water Dropwort behind; to walk on and look at the primroses which, I was assured, could be safely added to salads and eaten.

For the second part of the story, please keep the first part in mind! It was the same time of the year only two years later: late spring, early summer 2015. I was making my way from London to Devon to stay with Raphaela and visit my sons.

My strange experience began 30 miles from Bristol: I called Raphaela from a service station to say that I was on my way. She told me that she had booked into a workshop about tuning forks; that it was in Buckfastleigh, Devon, and started at 8pm. Did I want to go? I didn't really want to go to this workshop. I knew nothing about tuning forks and I was tired. But I didn't want to stop Raphaela from attending so I agreed providing that it worked out with timing.

I was amused to be so quickly swept up into the culture of Totnes, which is visionary and unexpected at times. I texted a friend, joking that I was going to a workshop on cutlery, saying that I would tell him what had happened.

In theory it should take me two and a half hours to arrive at Buckfastleigh by 8pm from the point at which I was travelling. It was now six o'clock. I didn't think that I was going to be able to make it.

I pulled out of the service station and onto the motorway: and seemed to enter into a time warp. I wasn't speeding; I didn't want to get a ticket. Somehow, and I have no idea how because it wasn't technically possible, at 8pm exactly I drew up in Buckfastleigh. Outside the Hall where the presentation on tuning forks was going to take place.

That evening I learned that a tuning fork is an acoustic

resonator in the form of a two-pronged fork with the prongs (tines) formed from a U-shaped bar of elastic metal (usually steel). Tuning forks are used for sound therapy tuning the body to achieve optimal physical balance. The practitioner said that the forks had been used to help cure various illnesses; had even helped with cancer. She invited everyone to try them out individually: I went first.

I could not bear the pitching of the tuning fork near my head; the practitioner had to work three feet away. She told me that I had had the most extreme reaction and was the most sensitive of anyone she had ever worked with. As soon as she started to 'play' the fork I recalled the Hemlock Water Dropwort: the energy felt most fey and most dangerous. I was being called away by fairy folk and elementals, all of whom were beseeching me to assist them; explaining to me that because humans have been taking so much from the Earth, we are tilting it out of balance. During the tuning my spirit was being called further and further away. The singing of the forks continued and I grew more and more afraid. I did not want to follow the sound. The nature spirits told me that henceforth I would be able to communicate with them more easily: they asked that I did not turn my back. In terms of the realignment, much needed to be done; bees especially are in great danger and that impacts on all of us.

My individual session finished. I was very shaken. I watched Raphaela have her turn; she had no problem in having the tuning forks right next to her head. Her reaction was totally different to mine. I did not mention to her what had happened to me until the next day. She told me that my aura had filled the room during the session: what was going on? I confessed to what had happened. She is wise in these matters, and said that I had been subject to an initiation, an awakening; that I should offer my assistance, as it had been asked for.

In all honesty I feel wary of working with elementals, nature spirits and fairy folk; like the Hemlock Water Dropwort I fear that their nature is fey and that I might be lost. Spirited away. I prefer to converse with Angels. It's much more straightforward! However, I accept this honor. I cannot pretend not to be open to their plight and ours: I am now walking upon our Earth as carefully as I can.

Chapter Ten

It was twelve noon on Sunday the 12th of April 2015. I was feeling quite content within myself as I parked on Tottenham Court Road, London WC1, and made my way down Charing Cross Road to Watkins Books on Cecil Court to spend the day Angel Channeling. I held my handbag securely in my hand as I went along: It contained my whole life.

I love Sundays in London because the congestion charge is lifted and there are places to park for free. As if I were a diplomat or VIP, I have the power and liberty of being able to sweep into the City in my car. I am afraid to admit it, but that day I put the needs of the nature spirits to one side: I know that it is more sensible and environmentally friendly to park just outside town and take the train in but I didn't listen to the voice of reason or sense.

I planned after work to collect my sons Josh and Zack in Devon going on to France for a holiday. The ferry was due to sail from Plymouth to Roscoff at 10pm on Monday the 13th of April; I could hardly wait. Steven my ex-husband was in also in London visiting his mother Helen; I had promised him a lift home. This was because he hadn't been well. The plan was to meet at Watkins at close of play and then drive to Devon.

I must admit that not only was I feeling content that day, I was also feeling a little bit smug; a part of me wanted Steven to see me at work in Watkins; that the transition made to another way of being had, despite many people's skepticism, borne fruit.

The day turned out very differently from the triumph that I had envisaged. At 7pm that evening I stood watching as a large hoist shaped like a hand picked up my battered little chariot of a car; swinging her gently onto a pickup truck; taking her out of the City. Like Cinderella her time was up.

At this point my pride had been stripped away; all I could hear was my Angel CB's voice in my ear. She was comforting me;

telling me, "All will be restored."

I have mentioned before how vulnerable I am when giving healing: not only am I channeling and open but I am literally halfway out of this world and halfway into the next. I am also totally focused on my client and on keeping them safe. That Sunday while I was working in Watkins my handbag disappeared. I do not know how it happened. Only that it did.

My handbag had been a joint birthday present from my Josh and Zack the year before. On this Sunday it had contained the following. My one and only car key, attached to a keyring that I loved everyday because it was a present from a dear friend. A pair of red leather gloves that I had bought for my mother for Christmas; they didn't fit her so she had sent them back to me. I didn't wear them that often but when I put them on they made me feel as if I was wearing Ruby Slippers, like Dorothy in *The Wizard of Oz*: a direct link through to home, they helped me to feel courageous. My passport. A purse that my ex-mother-in-law Helen had given me to help me be more organized, containing my driving license; photos of my sons, as well as my bankcards. An amethyst crystal that I used to demonstrate chi energy to clients and treasured for its beauty. A small piece of San Paulo wood, which I use to clear negative energy. Chromium capsules given with kindness by Dr. Mistry from South End Green to help stop sugar cravings so that I could lose weight. My hairbrush; an emery board; various receipts needed for my accounts; five pounds in cash. Scrunched up old tissues; a USB Stick holding a draft copy of this book.

The pickup truck took my car to a garage for £1000 worth of work, not only to replace the lock and have new keys fitted, but also to replace back brakes that I had not realized were worn out. I made my way to Paignton, Devon and my sons by train.

I was utterly furious with the person who took my handbag. I felt violated: I could feel their fingers combing through my possessions. It made me feel invaded. You may or may not have noticed but in many ways I consider myself to be a warrior. I don't hold much truck with some of the current conventions that say, "Oh the universe had other plans and everything happens for a reason." Or, "What did I do to attract this in to my life? It's all my fault." As far as I can see we all operate in a socioeconomic environment as well as a spiritual environment: sometimes decisions are made by others that impact upon us in ways that we cannot help. Sometimes things that happen upon us are beyond our control; we don't always need to internalize them, blame ourselves and work to rectify ourselves. It is not always about the law of attraction; other energies can be at play.

Despite my misgivings I was so traumatized by the handbag drama that I had to work with it to give myself peace; to sleep at night. Once my anger subsided I started to review what had happened. I gained some valuable insights. I saw that the theft was not personal: When I asked CB why had it happened I was shown the image of a flock of Seagulls. I saw that like Seagulls humans – including myself – have the capacity to demonstrate extraordinary grace; and that like Seagulls when we want or need resources, humans including myself have the potential to act in a predatory and callous manner.

Further I realized that I disliked elements of my own nature that I saw as predatory, and that this had made me disengage from the world. I did not want to be part of a screaming, uncontained, unthinking flock of birds hoovering up resources. Therefore I tended to opt out; I would give up or throw away resources rather than engage in a battle. Then CB was kind enough to show me the vision of a Hawk. I understood that I had it within me to try to behave in more of the manner of a Hawk: to rise above the clamor; to have clarity and exercise clear vision; to look ahead. To be contained and to be focused; to stay balanced; that I am entitled to resources ensuring on a day-to-day basis my needs are met. That there is a place for me in our world. That I have a right to be here; that I belong.

Epilogue

So did everything work out? Was it as CB had promised? Was all restored? One thing that I have learnt in this adventure is that whenever an Angel makes a promise they keep it. It may be a year or so out because Angels don't always understand about time, and it may occur in unexpected ways. Odd beat wing and prayer ways because Angels don't really understand how we use money; but to date all promises made have been kept, even if it sometimes has been according to the universe's interpretation of what is best for me rather than my own!

From Devon I continued to work on this book and carry out energy work to integrate myself. I also remembered that I had a long-forgotten pension tucked away; now I was 55 I could access it. I found a financial advisor skilled enough to manage the process for me; by 'coincidence' his mother happened to be a Reiki healer: he wasn't daunted by me, working efficiently to release the funds. Not vast amounts but just enough to set us back on our feet. Zack, Josh and I moved back to Totnes. So yes, our home was restored.

But it wasn't only about finances. I felt restored to myself by the sum of all my experiences; I had healed many wounds; carried out Tikkun Olam and repaired myself. For the first time in my life, after I returned home I no longer felt restless. In fact I felt the opposite: I felt that I wanted to come out of immersion in my story, into a place of peace and stability, without any more drama. For me holding this calmness; inner contentment; love and appreciation for my sons and friends; for my work – it truly feels that I am now experiencing Life as Grace.

I wasn't even tempted to ask CB for guidance as where to go next. In my entire portfolio of activities: energy healing, Angel channeling and intuitive coaching I am doing work that I love. I am living Magically, in Heaven on Earth. Then I received an unexpected surprise; bizarrely everything was restored, exactly as CB had said it would be, even the consultancy work. On the very day that I submitted the final draft of this book to my editor Leah, a colleague e-mailed me and asked if I wanted to join their consultancy practice on a part-time basis. I accepted. I can see that, as CB had told me, the Spiritual and the Material integrate. There is no divide.

Thank you for accompanying me on my Journey. I hope that my story is helpful and serves you. Shine well and happy traveling to you and your Angel(s).

References and Bibliography

Preface
1. Ursula Le Guin, *The Earthsea Quartet*, Penguin, reprint edition (24 June 1993)

Part One: Ordinary Life
1. *Kohelet* from Ecclesiastes 3:1–8
2. www.radicalforgiveness.com
3. Bi-Aura Energy Healing is an advanced system of bio-energy healing which works through balancing the human bio-field. More information may be found at www.bi-aura.com.
4. http://www.mikel.tv/funkymonkey

Part Two: Transition
1. Chakras are the body's energy centers through which the life force flows helping to maintain physical, mental, emotional and spiritual balance. First identified in India – the word Chakra is derived from the Sanskrit word for wheel.
2. Attributed to Gandhi.
3. Local Exchange Trading Schemes (LETS) and Credit Unions. LETS are a community system of mutual support and exchange that may be used without exchanging money. Credit Unions are Community Banks.
4. Volume 1: *The Zohar*, Beresheet A Noach, published by the Kabbalah Centre International Inc. First Print 2001; Revised Edition 2003.
5. Doreen Virtue and Lorna Byrne are contemporary Angel experts and authors.
6. Raphaela Cooper, Artist, may be contacted by: email@seraphise.plus.com
7. John Levine: http://www.silenceofmusic.com

8. American author Maya Angelou (4.4.28–28.5.14): I have been unable to find a reference for this widely known quote that is attributed to her.

9. Source: www.physics.org

10. www.thebeegoddess.com

11. Barbel Mohr, *Cosmic Ordering: The Next Step*, Hay House UK (7 September 2009)

12. Boe Huntress, Singer, Songwriter and Shakti dance teacher may be contacted at: http://www.boehuntress.com/contact.html

13. Marianne Williamson, *A Return to Love: Reflections on the Principles of a Course in Miracles*, Thorsons, New Ed edition (18 November 1996)

14. *Forms of Prayer for Jewish Worship*, Edited by the Assembly of Rabbis of the Reform Synagogues of Great Britain. Publisher: Reform Synagogues of Great Britain; 7th edition (September 1977)

15. Schumacher College in Dartington, Devon. https://www.schumachercollege.org.uk

16. *Wild Love*, Gill Edwards, Piatkus, Reprint Edition (29 March 2012)

17. *Carl Jung: Wounded Healer of the Soul, an Illustrated Biography*, Claire Dunne, Watkins Publishing (2012)

18. http://www.ted.com/talks/simon_sinek_how_great_leaders_inspire_action?

19. Jenna Lilla: www.jennalilla.com

Part Three: Extraordinary Life

1. *Oxford Dictionary & Thesaurus* (Oxford University Press, 2001)

2. *Kindred Spirit Magazine*: www.kindredspirit.co.uk

3. http://www.vday.org

4. Awakening of Love: http://www.pathoflove.net/programs/awakening_of_love

About the Author and contact details

Before becoming an Angel Channeler, Energy Healer and Intuitive Coach, Wendy Jane Erlick worked to promote equalities and excellence in Local Government in England for twenty-five years. She is a Blogger and has had articles published in *Kindred Spirit* magazine. This is her first book. Wendy lives in Totnes, Devon, with her family. You can be in touch with Wendy by e-mail at wendyjaneerlick@gmail.com. If you would like to book an appointment with Wendy you may find information on how to do this at her Blog: https://celestialhealing.wordpress.com. It is also possible to book an appointment with Wendy through Watkins Books: details below.

About Watkins Books and contact details

Watkins Books is an esoteric bookshop in the heart of London. Established over 100 years ago, we are now one of the world's leading independent bookshops specializing in new, secondhand and antiquarian titles in the Mind, Body, Spirit field. Watkins import books from around the world including America and India, and staff are all experts in one or more themes in the shop, so you can ask them for recommendations and advice. Located right in the middle of London's "Theatreland", Watkins Books is very easy to reach and find. Coming by tube the closest stop is **Leicester Square (Northern and Piccadilly lines)**: take a Charing Cross Road exit and turn in the direction of Trafalgar Square. After a short walk you will find Cecil Court on your left and the shop is halfway down this famous pedestrian alley. Address: **19-21 Cecil Court, London WC2N 4EZ**.

Watkins is open 7 days a week! Mon, Tue, Wed & Fri: 10.30am–6.30pm; Thu & Sat: 11am–7.30pm; Sundays: 12–7pm. Call +44 (0)20 7836 2182.

About the Book Editor and contact details

Leah Kotkes, MA is a published writer and writing mentor to new and advanced writers working on books and magazine articles. She is a former magazine editor, features writer and newspaper columnist. She began her journalist career as a broadcast journalist. Formerly, she worked in book publishing and has worked also as a publicist and marketing consultant.

Currently, she lives in London. She studies part-time at the University of Oxford where she is reading English Literature.

Contact: leahkotkes@gmail.com.

B O O K S

O is a symbol of the world, of oneness and unity; this eye represents knowledge and insight. We publish titles on general spirituality and living a spiritual life. We aim to inform and help you on your own journey in this life.

Visit our website: http://www.o-books.com

Find us on Facebook:
https://www.facebook.com/OBooks

Follow us on Twitter: @obooks